Darkness to Light

Psalm 27: One Man's Journey Toward Wholeness

Danny Mullins

ISBN-13: 978-0615948676
ISBN-10: 0615948677

Dedication

This book is dedicated to my grandsons,
Jonathan and Nathan.
You were lights of hope in my dark days.

Contents

Foreword

Danny Mullins has been my friend for fifteen years. We lived for a while in the same neighborhood, on the same block, on the same side of the street, just a few doors away without ever meeting or saying a word to each other. We would have continued happily without ever emerging from our respective caves had it not been for his wife, who learned that I was a Lutheran pastor and thought it might be nice for her Pentecostal, worship-leading husband and I to meet. Such are the inconspicuous beginnings of lifelong bonds.

Along the way Danny and I would share ministries, movies, and the occasional single malt, enjoying each other's company and trading theological perspectives. In all the years I've known Danny, though, I did not see the dark corridors he was walking. He kept his inner turmoil private, the way men do, and did his best to make the best of things.

But we can only go so far trying to make the best of things. Sooner or later our depletion becomes total, the walls cave in, and the lights go out.

That's what happened to Danny.

This book is his public account of how bitter experiences pushed him toward wholeness. The greatest value of this book lies in its bald, matter-of-fact narration of the dark places of our inner lives and the lunatic self-management of our emotional prisons. "One consequence of my increasing inner darkness was that I had become blind to my emotional condition," he says of his own prison. "Emotional brokenness is a two-edged sword. Not only will it cause your blindness, it will also prevent you from being aware of your blindness. I had lost touch with how I honestly felt about myself, about God, and about those around me."

Here, in the straightforward description of these bleak and life-stealing conditions, is to be found much of the greatness of this book. It is a warm and human challenge of our inability to fix ourselves and a hope-filled declaration of the innate kindness of God in doing for us what we cannot possibly do for ourselves.

This book is real. It is true. It is not imaginative fiction. It emerges out of bitter tears amid the cruelties and vagaries and complexities of human existence in a fallen world. These things are incontestably a part of life. They exist. We experience them. But there is a way forward, a way beyond, a way through. This book points to that way—an authentic way of fierce submission to God's relentless goodness and passionate care for us. As you read, may God surprise you along that way.

Graeme Sellers, Pastor
Wonderful Mercy Church‾
Gilbert, Arizona

Post tenebras lux
After Darkness, Light

In the sixteenth century, this phrase was adopted
as the motto of the Protestant Reformation.
It is engraved on the Reformation Wall in
Geneva, Switzerland.

Introduction

The Darkness

It's the darkest dark you can imagine. In fact, you can't imagine it, at least I couldn't. Deprived of your sense of sight, you are robbed of all perspective. Movement has no meaning because it can't be detected. In most contexts of darkness, the passing of time allows for an adjustment of vision. Not so in the darkness I am describing. The absence of light is total. All points of reference are lost. It is a darkness that is palpable and somehow alive. It wraps its cloak around every area of your life and you are left alone with yourself.

In the southeastern corner of New Mexico lies a geological marvel known as Carlsbad Caverns. It is a labyrinth of spectacular subterranean chambers that snake their way deep beneath the New Mexican desert. I have visited the caverns several times throughout my life. The park contains 117 caves. They house some of the most dramatic geological formations in the world. Thus far, 126 miles of caverns have been mapped and explored; the deepest reaches a depth of 1640 feet below the earth's crust. It is the deepest limestone cavern in the United States. The largest room lies 750 feet below the surface and covers a little over eight acres with a ceiling height reaching 350 feet. The park averages almost five hundred thousand visitors a year. Guided tours offered throughout the day provide an opportunity to explore the massive complex of caves, tunnels, pits, and pools. At some point in the tour, once you are deep below the earth's surface, the lights are turned out. The guide informs you ahead of time so you can prepare yourself. You are instructed to find a spot, be still, take a deep breath, and relax, but I'm not sure you can prepare yourself for the degree of darkness that engulfs you. You cannot see your hand directly in front of your face. It's the blackest black I have ever experienced.

March 2012

The awareness of my personal darkness came early in the spring. In reality, the lights had been out for quite some time. Much like my experience in the caverns, it was something for which I was totally unprepared. I had never had an experience to match it nor ever expected to. It was as though an oppressive gloom had sucked all the air from the room. I was suffocating. Under normal circumstances you never consciously think about breathing, yet every breath I took seemed to require great effort. I was fighting for my life. I lost all points of emotional reference. I no longer possessed perspective. Like a blind man with a cane, I tapped my way through life day after day. I took my clues for living from those around me, for I seemed to have lost the ability to understand what it meant to live. I existed. I survived. I did not, however, live.

Unlike my experience at the caverns, the darkness in which I found myself was not the result of a sudden event. No one had flipped off the switch. My darkness had been years in the making, though I was completely unaware of it at the time.

I had unknowingly been on a descending emotional path for a very long time. I did not see it coming, though the warning signs were there. Numbness had crept in like a slow paralysis. My reaction to traumatic events was an abnormal calmness. I deceived myself by viewing my reaction as peace from God in the middle of a storm. It was no such thing. I was emotionally out of touch and becoming more so as time passed. I was the proverbial frog in the pot of gradually warming water. I was cooked before I knew it and unable to jump out of the pan. Unlike the cavern tour, there was no warning by a guide. No opportunity to get my bearings. No chance to prepare for the blackness that exploded upon me. The lights simply went out.

The Roots of Darkness

Emotional pain, if ignored and untended, is debilitating. Such was the beginning of my journey into the cave, the genesis of my descent. Emotional woundedness is a disease that, when left unchecked, will negatively impact every area of your life. Leaving deep soul pain unattended is not a neutral proposition. We can refuse to acknowledge it exists, deny anything ever happened, claim what did happen was not really that big of a deal, cover it in a cloak of humor, man or woman-up and put on a show of strength, or hide behind a veneer of religious clichés, but the consequences of unaddressed emotional pain cannot be avoided. As a child I did not know how to deal with the hurts I suffered. As a teenager, I used the energy and busyness of youth to distance myself from my emotional brokenness. I deprived myself of any time to think about it by never slowing down. Through the years, I learned unhelpful and unhealthy ways of coping with the unavoidable pain that is part of the world in which we live. By not dealing with my hurts, I created a pain pileup, a freeway accident that kept getting worse as the next car came over the hill oblivious to what lay ahead. The ignorance of my condition coupled with an unacknowledged unwillingness to face a painful past eventually caught up with me. The lights went out.

Each of us reacts differently to bottled-up emotional pain. Anger is an all too common response. The least little thing sets us off. Usually it is not the present thing to which we are actually reacting. The level of anger is generally completely out of proportion to what just happened. The current incident is simply the fuse igniting the explosive hurt of past years. Bitterness is also a common expression of unhealed pain. It is a sour disposition that finds nothing good in any situation. Those who funnel their hurt through that outlet are miserable to keep company with. The Bible likens bitterness to a root that, when breaking through the soil, troubles, defiles, and corrupts everyone within reach (Heb. 12:15). Similarly, the Blame Game is a coping option for the walking wounded. If it's not our fault, we don't have to do anything about it; yet, we are the ones who suffer the often lifelong repercussions of that decision. Blaming almost inevitably leads to a life of unforgiveness, something Jesus has strong words against. The failure to forgive from the heart bears the consequence of not being forgiven (Matt. 6:15). Withdrawal is another strategy employed. If we pull away from everything and everyone, perhaps pain can be avoided. That plan proves to be a pipe dream. It has never worked and it never will. Isolation simply leaves us alone with our pain. It doesn't deal with it. Practiced as a lifestyle, these various attempts at pain management lead deeper and deeper into the cave. Unless another path is chosen, it will result in a darkness that will rob us of our lives. In the increasingly dimming light, the path will disappear and we will lose our way.

To a greater or lesser degree I have been guilty of practicing each of these coping strategies. The particular concoction I brewed from these ingredients led me on a journey that ended in clinical depression. Depression is a thief.

It robs you of things that rightfully belong to you, things you were meant to possess: joy, peace, hope, and a sense of wellbeing. If there is an absence of these in your life, this book is written for you. Though the result of your failure to deal with the pain in your life may not have resulted in clinical depression, it is leading you toward the same place of darkness it led me. Any strategy to manage your emotional pain other than the healing presence of Jesus and his word will eventually and surely fail. Most certainly we experience pain, grief, frustration, and loss in this life, but those are not our home. They are experiences from which we recover. We were never intended to live in a perpetual state of pain and hopelessness. My failure to recover resulted in clinical depression.

My experience grew from the soil of my own life, not from someone else's. It was a soil sown with wrong choices based on misshapen beliefs about God and myself. One of my purposes for writing is to make others aware of the warped perspectives I had adopted and hopefully help them avoid making similar destructive choices that lead to a place of emotional, spiritual, and physical exhaustion. This is what the absence of light does to you, what it did to me: it wears you down. When the light goes out, it doesn't simply shut down the capacity for sight. A fundamental characteristic of the darkness is confusion. Consequently, in the dark you don't think as clearly. You have no true sense of where you are or where you might be headed. Darkness engenders directionless living, which proves to be a frustrating and exhausting way to exist.

In my weariness, I could keep my eyes open no longer. I fell asleep, but not in a good way. It was the sleep of death. God, in his grace, woke me from my deadly slumber. No one is immune from what I experienced. To imagine you are is to invite the possibility. John the Baptist's father prophesied at his son's birth, *"Because of our God's merciful compassion, the Dawn from on high will visit us to shine on those who live in darkness and*

12

the shadow of death, to guide our feet into the way of peace" (Luke 1:78-79 HCSB). Zechariah's words express my hope for each reader of this book: the rescue of those for whom the light has gone out and the safeguarding of those whom the darkness has not yet ensnared.

The Anchor

During my time in the cave, Psalm 27 became a great source of restorative hope and healing. Every aspect of the song spoke in life-affirming ways to me. This book is an account of my life with this psalm. It was my biblical home for over a year. At various points in my past, I have practiced journaling; never, however, for long periods of time. I usually employed it in times of stress or crisis to help me process what I was going through. My hope was it would help me clarify the correct questions and discern the right answers. Sometimes, however, it simply became an opportunity to vent. Venting in print can serve a useful purpose. Better ink on paper than angry words verbally flung at others, words you usually wish had never escaped your lips. Sometimes, however, journaling simply deteriorates into venomous vomit which isn't good for anyone, the writer included. Thankfully, in my case, those words never saw the light of anyone's day but mine.

I had a concern that my present journaling was declining into just such a pit. I became worried it would simply increase, as opposed to help alleviate, the depressed state I was in, so I made a choice. In hindsight, it was a God-breathed choice. I decided to spend my journaling time reflecting on Psalm 27. That choice proved to be an anchor that stopped the spiritual and emotional drift within which I was caught. It gave me the strength to take the necessary steps to reverse the course of my life and rediscover the pleasure of

God, the pleasure he took in me, and the life he had created me to live.

The following collection of thoughts and meditations came out of my darkness. David declares in Psalm 139, *"Even in darkness I cannot hide from you. To you the night shines as bright as day. Darkness and light are the same to you"* (Ps. 139:12). Thankfully, my darkness was not God's darkness. On the contrary, in the end his light became my light. Through the words of Psalm 27, his light began to shine upon the path of my life. I followed his gradually increasing light out of the cave in which I was trapped. I followed it until I emerged into the brilliant light of day. I pray you will find in David's words the light, the life, the hope, and the strength I found. I believe, in fact, you will find much more in the fourteen verses of this psalm than I did, for there is much more than I have uncovered. May the words, truths, declarations of faith, the appeals for acceptance, the fears honestly expressed, the prayers earnestly prayed, the enemies squarely faced, and the encouragement of hope that rose from David's heart be a lighted path that will lead you out of any darkness you may be experiencing. I believe the same light I found in David's words will light your way to a life of healing and wholeness.

Psalm 27

(A psalm of David)

¹ *The Lord is my light and my salvation— so why should I be afraid?*
The Lord is my fortress, protecting me from danger, so why should I
tremble?
² *When evil people come to devour me, when my enemies and foes*
attack me, they will stumble and fall.
³ *Though a mighty army surrounds me, my heart will not be afraid.*
Even if I am attacked, I will remain confident.
⁴ *The one thing I ask of the Lord— the thing I seek most— is to live in*
the house of the Lord all the days of my life, delighting in the Lord's
perfections and meditating in his Temple.
⁵ *For he will conceal me there when troubles come; he will hide me in*
his sanctuary. He will place me out of reach on a high rock.
⁶ *Then I will hold my head high above my enemies who surround me.*
At his sanctuary I will offer sacrifices with shouts of joy, singing and
praising the Lord with music.
⁷ *Hear me as I pray, O Lord. Be merciful and answer me!*
⁸ *My heart has heard you say, "Come and talk with me." And my*
heart responds, "Lord, I am coming."
⁹ *Do not turn your back on me. Do not reject your servant in anger.*
You have always been my helper.
Don't leave me now; don't abandon me, O God of my salvation!
¹⁰ *Even if my father and mother abandon me,*
the Lord will hold me close.
¹¹ *Teach me how to live, O Lord. Lead me along the right path, for my*
enemies are waiting for me.
¹² *Do not let me fall into their hands. For they accuse me of things I've*
never done; with every breath they threaten me with violence.
¹³ *Yet I am confident I will see the Lord's goodness while I am here in*
the land of the living.
¹⁴ *Wait patiently for the Lord. Be brave and courageous. Yes, wait*
patiently for the Lord.

Chapter One

The Light

"The Lord is my light and my salvation…"
Psalm 27:1

David's first words in this psalm are the echo of creation across the ages of time, *"Let there be light…and there was light."* It is a law of nature; darkness dissipates in the presence of light. It was light that initiated my re-creation. In my season of darkness, David's words, God's words through him, became my words, a personal declaration of faith, a ray of hope. *"The Lord is my light."* Despite what I felt, despite what I did or did not see, over the course of months these words passed my lips over and over again, *"The Lord is my light."* The effect was not instantaneous, but gradually I began to sense the Day Star dawning in my heart. *"The Lord is my light."* The horizon began to lighten. I glimpsed the beginnings of a new day.

Eye Problems

Black is the opposite of white. Day is the opposite of night, but darkness is *not* the opposite of light. Darkness is the absence of light. Unlike my experience in the depths of Carlsbad Caverns, the cause of my darkness was not due to someone flicking off a switch. In that instance, someone deprived me of light. In my instance, I deprived myself of light. For years my sight had been fading. I simply hadn't realized it. It wasn't a darkness that threatened the loss of my salvation. My salvation was never in jeopardy. If I had died in the depths of my depression, an appealing option at more than one point, I would have been welcomed into the loving arms and smiling face of Jesus. The problem had to do with vision and perception, both of which are key elements in determining your quality of life. The problem was with my eyes, the eyes of my heart. *"Lord we want to see."* This was the response of the two blind beggars to Jesus' question regarding what they wanted (Matt. 20:29-33). Like the beggars, I lived in a world of darkness. My cry for mercy mirrored theirs. I wanted to see again.

One consequence of my increasing inner darkness was that I became blind to my emotional condition. Emotional brokenness is a two-edged sword. Not only will it cause your blindness, it will also prevent you from being aware of your blindness. I had lost touch with how I honestly felt about myself, about God, and about those around me. How you *ought* to feel and how you *actually* feel can be, and often are, two very different things. I grew up in a world of *oughts*. How I ought to feel and act as determined by those around me became the guiding principles for my life. I had allowed others to define who I was and the path I should walk. They were no doubt well-meaning attempts at helping me along my way. Many of them were sound and full of wisdom, though not all would have qualified as such. In the religious world in which I grew up, however, there was no room for disagreement. An honest dissenting opinion was neither sought nor encouraged. Rather, it was often punished. Loyalties were questioned and, if you persisted, stigmas were attached. For that reason I, for the most part without question, accepted the established standards of my environment as my own. The consequence of this acceptance combined with my attempts to conform and gain the acceptance of others resulted in the submersion of who I was beneath a mountain of obligation and performance. The problem, however, was not with others but with me. The responsibility for my lack of insight rested solely with me. Accepting responsibility for that fact is a key step in moving out of any darkness you may find yourself in. At some point, I failed to make the transition from being led by others, appropriate at certain stages of life, to being led by my own heart. I believe I had lost the ability to see. When you cannot see, you lose all confidence in your ability to move about. I was living in a darkness of my own making. In that darkness, I placed myself at the mercy of others in regards to the path of my life.

There is a great paradox in all of this. As I look back, I realize I was standing in the light the entire time. God had not forsaken me, Jesus was still present, and the Holy Spirit remained close. I was standing in the light, but with my eyes closed. My personal experience was one of darkness. I was standing in the light and living in the dark. Why would someone do that? Live in the light with your eyes closed? It wasn't done on purpose. It began with a gradual slide down a slippery slope. I was, however, unaware the slope was slick. In hindsight, my ignorance comes as no surprise. Each of us inherited a susceptibility to deception. Eve, our first mother, is intimately acquainted with how deception can appear to be truth, how darkness can pass itself off as light.

David prays, *"Keep me from lying to myself"* (Ps. 119:29). For me, the deception began by viewing the events of my life through my own lens, a lens that had been clouded by painful experiences. Instead of viewing them through the lens of God's word, I viewed them from my own perspective, a perspective that had been warped by the emotional damage I had suffered. Adopting my perspective and interpretation of the things I had experienced and imagining it to be God's perspective was a recipe for disaster. Isaiah advises and then warns, *"If you are walking in darkness without a ray of light, trust in the Lord and rely on your God. But watch out, you who live in your own light and warm yourselves by your own fire. This is the reward you will receive from me. You will soon fall down in great torment"* (Isa. 50:10b-11). I had allowed my light to take precedent over God's. My light, my understanding of things, proved to be darkness. I had warmed myself by my own fire, an image which speaks of the things we use to comfort ourselves. Through the years, I had turned to many things other than the Lord for comfort. To be honest, some of them provided a temporary measure of relief but nothing that endured. Why would any of us do that? Often it is because the truth is too difficult to bear at the moment. It's less painful to believe a lie. Sometimes our pride prevents us from seeing and acknowledging the truth because of what doing so would say about who we are as a person. It would threaten the false image of ourselves that we have clung to and reveal the ugly parts we feared were present. Rather than face that possibility, I preferred to comfort myself with many of the multitude of options our society affords. Soon the slope was so slippery the slide was unrecoverable. I picked up speed without even trying. I became the proverbial snowball rolling down the hill, gaining mass and momentum by the minute. Like Dorothy of Oz and her companions crossing the poppy fields on their way to the Emerald City, I had run until I could run no longer. My eyes closed in the sleep of death. I lost sight of where I was going.

One of the primary culprits in my demise was the disease of disillusionment, a sickness which had gradually, like arthritis, crept into my life making every movement a painful effort. Everyone experiences trouble, pain, suffering, and loss. It's an inescapable part of living in the world. Our response to that pain, perhaps more than any other single thing, determines the quality of the life we will live. My life became defined by the pain stemming from the traumas I experienced from my childhood to the present. The sands of hope had been slipping through my hour glass at such a rate there was more space than sand in the cylinder. I developed an increasing expectation of disappointment. A blanket of doubt settled upon the shoulders of my heart, doubt regarding what I thought I knew, what I thought I believed. My eyelids grew heavy and were incrementally closing. Eventually, they shut completely and darkness consumed my soul. Jesus said *"Your eye is a lamp that provides light for your body. When your eye is good, your whole body is full of light. But when your eye is bad, your whole body is filled with darkness"* (Matt 6:22-23a). My life was a poster child for what happens when your eye is bad.

Paul's Blindness

Though there are certainly some major differences in my situation and that of the Apostle Paul, there are also some striking similarities. Saul of Tarsus, pre-Paul, was going about life as his duties demanded. He had, as had I, accepted the established standards of his day. He was, however, deeply deceived. He was operating out of a place of religious darkness. It resulted in outright opposition to the very thing God was doing. The Messiah he was looking for, the Light of the World, had arrived and Saul found himself working in direct opposition to God. Oddly, when the Light broke into Paul's life on the road to Damascus it resulted in a physical darkness that changed the course of his life. The darkness he experienced shook him to the core of his being. He became open to seeing things in a way he was previously unwilling to do. He emerged from his time of darkness with a new perspective, fresh vision, and a divinely inspired purpose. In hindsight, his blindness proved to be a great blessing. Similarly, as I look back at my own season of blindness I do so with a heart of thanksgiving. My life has been radically changed as a result of my experiences. Just as Paul did not find healing without the love and involvement of others, my story reads the same. Healing prayers prayed by faithful family members and friends played a key role in my own deliverance. A time of darkness can be the result of our own doing or, as in Paul's case, the intervention of God. Whatever the case, God can and will use our experience with darkness to open our eyes to his eternal, light-filled purposes.

Except for divine intervention, I would still be laying in the poppy fields of Oz. Except for divine intervention, the blind beggars of Jericho would have remained sightless. The beggars' cry for mercy was heard and the compassionate healing of Christ enveloped them. My cry for mercy, as well, did not go unheeded. Unlike the Jericho blind men, my healing was not instantaneous but it was no less miraculous. God descended on my life with the rain of his healing presence and my eyes began to open.

Why not a sudden breakthrough? Why not, as in the depths of the New Mexican desert, the flipping of a switch and the immediate appearance of light? Why not instantaneous illumination? Why not, as the blind men of Jericho, an immediate restoration of sight? Perhaps it has happened like that for some. I can tell you my eyes opened more quickly than the years it took them to close, a fact for which I am extremely grateful. It was for me, however, a gradual process and not an event.

The Power of the Word

The opening words of the psalm ring daily in my ears. *"The Lord is my light."* They remain an integral part of my everyday walk with Christ. I believe they always will. Don't be discouraged if at first you only see men walking about as trees (Mark 8:24). Don't lose hope if you do not have the clarity you desire as quickly as you think you should have it. Be assured the hand of Jesus will remain extended toward you until your vision clears and the joy of seeing returns. Though it took a season of time, God's reality became my reality, God's perspective became my perspective. I stand again in his presence with open eyes. The Emerald City glows in the distance and I once again run with abandon toward the vision of the King and his Kingdom. Hope has returned. Vision grows. Strength for the journey increases.

I cannot overestimate the power of God's word and the undeniable and indispensable role it played in my journey from darkness to light. The writer of Hebrews declares, *"The word of God is alive and powerful. It is sharper than the sharpest two-edged sword, cutting between soul and spirit, between joint and marrow. It exposes our innermost thoughts and desires. Nothing in all creation is hidden from God"* (Heb. 4:12-13a). The words of David as breathed by the Holy Spirit brought life and resurrection power to the deepest parts of my being. It pierced and divided my soul. It separated me from the lies I had embraced and rescued me from the resulting despair those lies had produced. I pray you find great truth, strength, and healing through the words of David, but if not this psalm then some other passage of God's word that he providentially brings to your life. Begin to allow the truth of God's word to rise in your heart, be breathed through your lungs, be shaped by your lips, and uttered by your voice in the midst of your own darkness. *"The Lord is my light and salvation."* May the words of God become an indelible part of your being that

nothing can erase. His words have the power to heal your
blindness, open your eyes, and restore your soul.

Chapter Two

Losing Yourself

"...so why should I be afraid?"
Psalm 27:1

More than seven billion people currently live on earth. Scientists estimate that throughout the course of human history over one hundred billion people have called our planet home. The latter number is obviously a scientific projection. Only the one who numbers the hairs of our head has an accurate count. Whatever the actual number, it is astonishing to consider that two identical human beings have never existed. Our individual uniqueness is a wonder of God. It is only one aspect of the limitlessness within which he lives and acts. Simone de Beauvoir said, "To be oneself, simply oneself, is so amazing and utterly unique an experience that it's hard to convince oneself so singular a thing happens to everybody."[1] And yet it does. It is the reason why the loss of any single individual life is a loss for us all. There is only one of each of us. In any market I am acquainted with, that would make us priceless. C. S. Lewis, in his famous sermon *The Weight of Glory*, states, "There are no *ordinary* people. You have never talked to a mere mortal."[2] Lewis had a keen awareness of the inestimable value of a single human soul. We are all immortal beings living out for a period of time a segment of our existence in this temporal world. Someday our mortal existence will end with the death of our bodies and we shall continue to exist in an eternal state whose God-designed nature is still unclear to us. We can, however, deprive God and each other of who we are without physically dying. Once the innocence of Eden was forfeited we became broken people living in a broken world. We've been attempting to pick up the pieces ever since. We can, as the prodigal son, lose our way and possibly lose ourselves.

My greatest regret is that somewhere along my journey, rather than recover my life, I lost it. As the light in which I lived slowly decreased, I began losing sight of the person God created me to be. Parker Palmer says, "It is indeed possible to live a life that is other than one's own."[3] It is entirely possible to act like someone other than who you actually are. The real you still resides within your being, but it can become buried beneath the pain and debris of life. It's easy to lose track of things when you're emotionally hurting. Pain can blind us to God's reality regarding our lives. When you're hurting, it's easy to be distracted. It's easy to forget who you are and what belongs to you. Forgetting who you are and what is yours can result in the most devastating of losses. It can result in failing to live the life you were destined to live and settling for less than the person you were divinely designed to be. The story of the prodigal son graphically illustrates my point. Born as the son of a wealthy man, destined to walk in his father's footsteps, he chose a path that resulted in the loss of all he had. He woke up one morning feeding pigs in a foreign land. It was not who he was or what he was called to be doing but he had, nevertheless, arrived at the pigpen.

It's easier to wind up in the pigpen than you might imagine. It often begins with believing a lie about yourself that parades about as the truth. The lie can be one of either overestimating or underestimating who you actually are. The former leads to an arrogance that Proverbs says precedes a destructive fall (Prov. 16:18). The latter, often a deceptive, false humility, leads to a paralyzing fear that imprisons the person God created us to be. Faced with possession of the Promised Land, the Israelites viewed themselves as grasshoppers before the opposition (Num. 13:33). Their underestimation cost that generation possession of what God had promised them. We can arrive at the pigpen by allowing fear and shame to prevent us from acknowledging our weaknesses for what they are and allowing God's grace and strength to be the backbone of our lives. Attempts at living life in our own strength will be disastrous. Paul declared that when he was weak was the actual moment of strength in his life (2 Cor. 12:10). To lose yourself is to lose a sense of purpose. Purpose is as essential as the air we breathe. Dallas Willard, in his book *The Divine Conspiracy*, says, "We were built to count, as water is made to run downhill. We are placed in a specific context to count in ways no one else does. That is our destiny."[4] In the fading light in which I was living, the purpose I previously had in my vision gradually dimmed from sight and with it the flame of life slowly extinguished within me. The pigpen was within sight.

Henri Nouwen said, "I am a prodigal son every time I search for unconditional love where it cannot be found."[5] Our losses create a poverty of spirit that makes us vulnerable to that which cannot help us. We find ourselves looking for affirmation and meaning in things that were never intended to provide it. We desperately search for a sense of well-being, a settled peace, and a joy that endures. Often the best we can do is the temporary distraction provided by satiating our thirst at the many wells of pleasure the world offers. We become shopaholics, alcoholics, or workaholics as we seek to satisfy the gnawing emptiness within. Yet, the entire time there is bread in the Father's house. *"...so why should I be afraid?"* Why should I be afraid that God doesn't know, or if he does know will not satisfy, the deepest needs of my life?

Just like the prodigal, it required devastating loss to bring me to my senses. The thing I lost was the most precious thing I had, the thing God had entrusted to no one else, the thing he had given solely to me: I lost myself. This understanding did not come all at once, just as the prodigal did not spend all his inheritance at once. It became slowly apparent over a period of time. Eventually, though, it was undeniable. The realization of what happened, that I had forfeited my life, devastated me. Jesus laments (Mark 8:36 NKJ), *"For what will it profit a man if he gains the whole world, and loses his own soul?"* I had not lost my soul in the sense of my salvation, I had lost my soul in the sense of the person God had created me to be. It was not as if I had sold my soul to Satan and signed the deed with my blood. Rather, throughout my life I had created a leaky bucket, a bag with holes in it. Things slipped away a little at a time. The thing that was slipping away was me, the real me, the me God had created for himself.

Through the years, I tried to become what others expected. One of my lifelong, glaring weaknesses has been that of people-pleasing, as if that was actually possible. I failed to dream my own dreams. I failed to think for myself. I failed to be honest with myself about myself. I failed to follow my own heart. People's affirmation, acceptance, and approval became more important to me than God's. I would never have admitted it was true, but I lived like it was true, because it was true. My unique God-given vision and purpose, in whatever ways I was in touch with it, took a back seat to that which others desired of me or told me I should be or do. I lost confidence in my own judgment. I was a leaf in the breeze, a wave of the sea driven by prevailing winds generated by others. I lost me.

The realization of what I was doing, what I had allowed to happen to me, was a great gift from God. A painful gift, but an extraordinary gift nonetheless. A Sufi poet once said the cure for the pain is the pain. Parker Palmer describes a similar experience, "After hours of careful listening, my therapist offered an image that helped me eventually reclaim my life. 'You seem to look upon depression as the hand of an enemy trying to crush you,' he said. 'Do you think you could see it instead as the hand of a friend, pressing you down to the ground on which it is safe to stand?'"[6] My depression did exactly that. It knocked all the props I had been using for years out from underneath me. Faulty foundations crumbled. Teetering walls collapsed. The pain of it all was the answer to the pain. I began to turn my face toward home. I began the search for the road back to the Father's house, the place where I was born, the source of my identity. Acknowledging a poverty of heart I had refused to see, I came face to face with my emotional bankruptcy. I was overdrawn and facing a debt I had no resources to deal with. Gary Kinnaman said of himself, "I was fallen from grace, not because I had committed some terrible sin, but because I was taking on life by myself."[7] Living life in your own strength, as opposed to living it by the grace of God, will eventually exhaust all your resources, and poverty of soul will overtake you. Your personal well runs dry. It is then you must remember where you came from and what belongs to you. There is bread in the Father's house. There is light in the Father's house. There is salvation in the Father's house. *"So why should I be afraid?"*

You cannot abdicate responsibility for your life. You cannot assign it to another human being. Fear can do that to you. It can rob you of the ability to be responsible before God for yourself and what he has entrusted to you. Luke 19:11-27 records Jesus' story of the ten servants. They were each entrusted with a sum of money. Their instructions during the absence of the master were to invest the money and earn a profit. Each of the ten, except for one, followed the master's instructions and earned, each according to his abilities, a return on the master's investment. The one servant, offering fear as his excuse, buried what he was given in the ground so that he would not lose it. The very thing he hoped to avoid was the very thing that happened. Upon the master's return, what he had been given was taken from him and given to someone else. The master reprimanded the fearful servant with these words, *"Risk your life and get more than you ever dreamed of. Play it safe and end up holding the bag"* (Luke 19:26 TM). I had buried my life in the ground. I was playing it safe. I was living someone else's version of my life. It's less risky. They can take the blame if things don't work out, or so you think. I am convinced living a life other than the one God has created you to live dishonors God. In the end it not only deprives you of what you have been given, it deprives God and the rest of the world of the gift that you are. As the words of Psalm 27 infiltrated the core of my being, something within me refused to be left "holding the bag." I felt as though my clay had lost its shape, but God, my creator, the wellspring of all that is good, stood ready to reshape the clay and once again blow his breath of life into me. It was time to get a shovel and remove what I had buried in the ground. One shovelful at a time it began to happen.

It is possible to recover your life. It is possible to remember what belongs to you. It is possible to come to your senses, turn your face toward home, and return to the place of your identity. You may have thus far squandered the resources that have been entrusted to you, but the essence of who you are remains. It may require devastating circumstances to bring you to your senses. The story of the prodigal reads, *"When he finally came to his senses, he said to himself, 'At home even the hired servants have food enough to spare,* *and here I am dying of hunger! I will go home to my father and say,* *"Father, I have sinned against both heaven and you, and I am no* *longer worthy of being called your son. Please take me on as a hired* *servant."' So he returned home to his father. And while he was still a* *long way off, his father saw him coming. Filled with love and* *compassion, he ran to his son, embraced him, and kissed him"* (Luke 15:17-20). The Father stands with outstretched arms, with nothing but love and grace to offer. Don't be afraid. A celebration awaits your return. It's time to remember who you are and what belongs to you. "What a long time it can take to become the person one has always been."[8]

When my race is run and my course is finished I would very much like them to say of me what they said of David. *For David, after he had served the purpose of God in his own* *generation, fell asleep, and was laid among his fathers, and* *underwent decay* (Acts 13:36 NASB). To serve the purpose of God in my generation, to live this life as God has destined me to live it, to leave behind the testimony of joyous completion. It is more than possible. It is the heart of God for each of us and he stands ready to aid us each step of the way. There is nothing to fear. There is bread in the Father's house. He waits, not in judgment, but with welcoming arms spread wide. No matter how dark it has been, cling to the words of David. *"The* *Lord is my light and my salvation – so why should I be afraid?"*

Now I become myself. It's taken time,
many years and places.
I have been dissolved and shaken,
worn other people's faces. [9]

Chapter Three

The Magic Button

"The Lord is my fortress, protecting me from danger, so why should I tremble?"
Psalm 27:1

Late at night, suitcase in hand, my dad is standing under the carport. He's leaving. My parents are separating. My mom, my brother, and I are standing in the kitchen door, the one that opens into the carport. Their separation eventually culminates in their first divorce. Everyone is crying. Not simply tears of pain, but agonizing sobs of gut-wrenching sorrow. That was the first time I pushed the magic button. I was six years old. I didn't know what else to do. It was an innate attempt at self-protection. When pain or trauma become too intense to bear, you have to do something in order to survive, so I pushed the button and the wall of emotional protection rose from somewhere deep within me and I distanced myself from the pain. Hypothetically, it's supposed to keep the pain out, to protect your heart. It can serve that purpose, not perfectly, of course, for there are side effects. Turns out it is a multi-functional wall, like it or not. Though the wall may act as a block for present pain, or at least most of it, it also locks past pain in. In addition to being a protective wall, it becomes a prison wall...and you're on the inside.

It wasn't a silver bullet. In fact, in the long run it had major downsides, but at the moment it helped. In my amateur button-pushing years, there was a measure of pain that squeezed in before I was able to get the wall up. My solution was to relegate the intruding pain to a prison cell to be managed as best I could. At least it was locked away somewhere, not running amok and causing all manner of trouble. Eventually, however, the prisoner always escapes. It's an imperfect plan for sure, but it was the only plan I had. Actually referring to it as a plan is generous. It wasn't a plan. I was playing it all by ear, instinctively reacting, seeking to avoid the deep heart hurts that were coming my way.

I got much better at button pushing. No longer an amateur, in the years that followed I could anticipate approaching pain with a fairly high degree of accuracy. I knew the signs. I became quick on the trigger, not unlike the best of gunslingers. I could hit the button in the blink of an eye. I could beat the pain to the punch, block the approaching blow but, as I have said, there are consequences to this particular method of pain management. The emotional distance you create between you and the pain is also created between you and the goodness of life you should be experiencing, between you and the people you should be close to, and ultimately between you and God.

This dysfunctional process is what brought my depression to a head. It was my feeble attempt to play God the Fortress, Protector from Danger, which brought me face to face with the foolishness of my choice to shoulder the burden for my safety. I make a very poor God. Through this passage in Psalm 27, I finally came to understand that my protection was never my responsibility. It has always been God's. He is described in Scripture as a wall of fire, a ring of mountains encircling, an encampment of angels surrounding, an impenetrable wall of salvation, a tower into which we can run and be safe, but it's tough to drop your guard after a half-century of raising it. It's tough to keep your finger off the button when you've spent your entire life keeping that button within finger's reach, but it's absolutely vital to the health of your soul that you resign as your personal protector. Perhaps the following will be a helpful plan as we seek to get out of the job we are so ill-fitted to fill.

Recognize

We must acknowledge what we have done and what we are continuing to do. It's critical that we own our choice to protect ourselves, that we accept personal responsibility for having done it. Oddly enough, that in and of itself can and probably will cause more pain, so be careful not to touch the button. In the end, it will be worth it. Perhaps I should be clear that I'm not talking about the healthy attribute of self-preservation given us by God. The next time you see a speeding bus headed your direction by all means step out of the way. It's God's will that you do so. I am speaking about taking upon ourselves a responsibility we were never meant to bear. David declares in Psalm 11:1, *"I trust in the Lord for protection."* Do we? Really? Are we able to drop our guard, to lower the walls we have built and allow the Lord to be responsible for the care of our lives emotionally, intellectually, spiritually, and physically?

"May the Lord answer you in the day of trouble; may the name of the God of Jacob defend you" (Ps. 20:1 NKJV). When troubles come, can we expect to be defended, or if we must

walk through troubles, can we trust him with the safety of our heart? It is no small decision. The interpretation of the events of our past might argue strongly that God has not done a very good job of protecting us. Yet, the scriptures are clear it is his job. *The Lord is my fortress, protecting me from danger, so why should I tremble?* Releasing the responsibility of our lives to God is the only way we will ever be free from living fear-filled lives. David declares (Ps. 20:1) that our defense is rooted in the name of God. Hundreds of years prior to David, Moses wrote (Deut. 32:1-4), *"Listen, O heavens, and I will speak! Hear, O earth, the words that I say! Let my teaching fall on you like rain; let my speech settle like dew. Let my words fall like rain on tender grass, like gentle showers on young plants. I will proclaim the name of the Lord; how glorious is our God! He is the Rock; his deeds are perfect. Everything he does is just and fair. He is a faithful God who does no wrong; how just and upright he is!"*

His name is like no other. Books have been written for the sole purpose of cataloging and understanding God's multifaceted name: Healer, Savior, Deliverer, Provider, God with Us, Prince of Peace, Almighty, Lord of Hosts, Shepherd, Righteousness. The list is endless, not surprising for a God without an end. Whatever we need, he is. It's all wrapped up in his name, a name David declares will defend us.

God can be trusted with our defense. If we will drop the wall, keep our fingers off the button, and allow him to do the job he has declared belongs to him, though we will not go through the remainder of our lives without experiencing pain, we will be kept safe within his immense hands, we will be secreted away in a crevice of the rock and his glory will be our protection.

Repent

Repentance is God's answer for every dysfunction that sin has created in our lives. Repentance reverses the direction of our hearts, and heads us down the right path. We may not know exactly where we are going, but repentance puts us on the right road to get there. It grants God access to our hearts. God opposes the proud, but gives grace to the humble. It positions us for healing grace to flow into the deepest recesses of our lives, the places of hidden, imprisoned, or unrecognized pain. Repent of assuming the responsibility for your own protection. Resign from the position. I would be lying if I said it wasn't a scary thing to do. The temptation to resume the role will rise again. A repeated repentance may prove to be necessary. If so, repent again. Every time you do, you distance yourself further and further from the role of defender. Eventually, you shall be able to say as David did, *"Truly my soul silently waits for God; from Him comes my salvation. He only is my rock and my salvation; He is my defense"* (Ps. 62:1-2 NKJV). David had such confidence in God as his defender his soul was able to wait in silence. That's quite a difference from a soul screaming in terror, assured that destruction is at the doorstep and convinced the pain threshold was surpassed some time ago. A soul that silently rests in the assurance of God's defense is remarkably rare, yet it is the way God has designed us to live. It is not only possible to live that way, it is God's purpose that we live that way. It pleases God's heart that we live that way. Repentance is the door that will lead us into a life of quiet rest based on an assurance of the unquestioned loving care of God for us and everything that has to do with us..."*so why should I tremble?"*

Receive

Receive God as your protector. It's always been his job. Perhaps someone along the way tried to teach us that. If they did, we didn't get it. We usurped God's job. Most of us did it unknowingly, without malicious intent, in childlike innocence. No one is to blame, but nonetheless we did it and it's time to stop. It's time to allow him to do what he is uniquely qualified and equipped to do, to be our protector. *"This is the kind of life you've been invited into, the kind of life Christ lived. He suffered everything that came his way so you would know that it could be done, and also know how to do it, step-by-step. He never did one thing wrong, Not once said anything amiss. They called him every name in the book and he said nothing back. He suffered in silence, content to let God set things right"* (1 Pet. 2:21-24 TM). Christ is uniquely qualified to defend us because he is the only human being who every moment of his life allowed God to be his defense. By refusing to protect himself, by accepting the pain that came his way Jesus transformed the world. Who knows what extraordinary thing might happen when we allow him to be the gatekeeper of our pain. *"The Lord is my fortress, protecting me from danger. So why should I tremble?"*

Chapter 4

Living in God's Reality

"When evil people come to devour me, when my enemies
and foes attack me, they will stumble and fall.
Though a mighty army surrounds me, my heart will not be afraid.
Even if I am attacked, I will remain confident."
Psalm 27:2-3

The presence and role of a spiritual enemy is obvious
to any serious reader of the Bible. From the book of Genesis to
John's Revelation, the enemy and his work are easily
discernible. I have always been aware of the opposition of a
cosmic foe, the battle between light and darkness, good and
evil, the kingdom of God versus the kingdom of Satan. That
being said, I was very slow in recognizing his work against me
in the emotional turmoil that eventually resulted in a diagnosis
of clinical depression. Once I did realize it, I was puzzled.

Why had it taken me so long? Why was I so blind to the hand of the enemy? In hindsight, his handiwork was very apparent.

While I do not believe every person suffering depression does so as a direct result of demonic attack, it would be equally fair to say I don't believe any depression comes from God. Satan's job description is concisely stated by Jesus in John 10:10, "*To steal and kill and destroy.*" Following this, Jesus describes his own mission: "*I have come that people may have life and have it in abundance.*" Having abundant, overflowing life is at the opposite end of the spectrum from depression. Depression steals your dreams, kills your ambitions, and destroys your hopes. Whether Satan is the source of depression or not, it is fertile ground for his activity. I was deep into the pit, however, before I recognized the participation of the enemy in what was happening to me. While seeking help for my depression, people had prayed in my presence against the enemy who was working against me. In counsel, people had spoken about the enemy's involvement in what was happening to me. I remember both of those things clearly. Yet the truth had somehow failed to register with me. I had not personally acknowledged or addressed the evil powers that, in hindsight, were obviously arrayed against me. It was David's words in Psalm 27 that awakened my heart and inspired and empowered me to take action.

"*When evil people come to devour me...when my enemies and foes attack me...*" The thought seemed preposterous to me. Evil people? Coming to devour me? Really? What had I ever done against them? Looking back, my questioning the attack is what now seems preposterous. What had I done to them? I had boldly declared the truth about God and his kingdom most of my life. I had publicly led and enthusiastically participated in gathered corporate worship that acknowledged Jesus as the high and exalted one. I had visited a number of nations across the world carrying the light of the gospel and the love of God. Nevertheless, I found myself surprised when enemies and foes attacked me. The activities I was involved in are simply those God had called me to participate in as a part of his family. The attack of the enemy comes equally as strong against any child of God who is actively engaged in serving the Father in whatever capacity he has called them. He will viciously attack any member of God's family who is engaged with pursuing God's heart and walking in obedience to his word. The presence of the enemy's work against me is now a foregone conclusion, a fact easily recognizable. However, at the time I seemed blind to it all.

Two of the enemy's key weapons are deception and minimization. The first I was thoroughly aware of as a weapon and had warned people against it. Adam and Eve fell as a direct result of deception. Minimization, however, had flown pretty low under my radar as incoming ordnance. Minimization is less obvious as an attack of the enemy. Did Adam and Eve imagine that their assigned task, that of tending the garden, was not a critical function, not very high on the ladder of cosmic importance? Did they undervalue and minimize their work and were therefore vulnerable to the enemy's deception? I don't know the answer. There is no biblical evidence to suggest it is true. I do know, however, that I minimized my God-given tasks and it left me in a vulnerable position. I had been lulled into believing what I did simply did not matter that much in the grand scheme of things. Perhaps you can identify with that feeling. I want to warn you against entertaining the thought for very long. In regards to sin, Martin Luther once likened it to a bird flying over your head. You can't keep the bird from flying over you but you don't have to allow it to build a nest on your head. Thoughts that minimize and devalue the person God has called you to be and the deeds he has called you to do must be immediately and soundly rejected. If you allow them to get a foothold in your thoughts and emotions, you will be granting the enemy access to your soul. He will build a nest and lay his eggs of deception that will eventually hatch into full grown lies. Those lies will derail you from the path God has carefully and lovingly planned for you.

I have read through Psalm 27 more times than I can count. However, once I acknowledged the work of the enemy in what was happening to me, I began to notice references to the enemy scattered throughout the psalm: *when evil people come to devour me...when my enemies and foes attack me...then I will hold my head high above my enemies who surround me...lead me along the right path for my enemies are waiting for me...don't let me fall into the hands of my enemy...they accuse me of things I have never done...with every breath they threaten me with violence.* I was shocked at the number of references to the enemy's active presence in these fourteen verses. I had treasured this psalm for much of my life, but it was because of other phrases: *The one thing I ask the Lord, the thing I seek the most...to live in his house forever...to meditate in his temple...*The Lord's invitation for David to *"Come and talk with me"* and David's response: *"I am coming"...I'm confident I'll see the goodness of the Lord in the land of the living.* Through the years, these and other verses in the psalm had been part of my worship and prayer life. I had failed, however, to see or perhaps purposely bypassed the consistent references to the enemy.

The deadliest mistake I made, the thing that most contributed to the onset of my depression, was viewing the trauma, loss, pain, and betrayal that had occurred in my life through my own eyes rather than God's, relying on my abilities to discern and interpret what was going on rather than discovering and allowing God's perspective of those events to rule the day. This choice became fodder for the enemy's grist mill. Jesus promised that in this world we would have trouble (John 16:33 NIV). When it occurs, why are we so surprised? Why was I so surprised? Trouble is unavoidable. The part over which we do have control is how we navigate trouble. What is the lens through which we choose to view what has happened? A little self-pity, a little resentment, a touch of bitterness, a pinch of despair, a failure to recognize the enemy's hand in it all, and the recipe for disaster had been mixed. I created a deadly stew from this foul combination of ingredients. It is what paved the path for my depression.

It was not, however, the final word on the subject. God had something to say about the work of evil and the attack of foes. God's words regarding the enemy have become precious to me, powerful words that reflect a reality I was completely out of touch with, words that have now become a part of the fiber of my being. They are not scripture passages that I quote but weapons that *have divine power to demolish strongholds...demolish arguments...and...take captive every thought to make it obedient to Christ* (2 Cor. 10:4-5 NASB).

> *"When evil people come to devour me,*
> *When my enemies and foes attack me*
> **They will stumble and fall.**
> *Though a mighty army surrounds me*
> **My heart will not be afraid**
> *Even if they attack me*
> **I will remain confident"**

It didn't *feel* like the enemy was stumbling and falling. My heart *was* afraid. I was *not* confident, but that was the perceived reality of a man with his eyes closed. The God who is light and lives in the light, his reality was something altogether different than mine. His reality was, *"They will stumble and fall...(your) heart will not be afraid...(you) will remain confident."* It was time to choose; God's reality or mine. I could hear the words of Joshua to the people of Israel, *"Choose today whom you will serve"* (Joshua 24:15). For me, it was more specifically *"Choose today whom you will believe."* It became obvious to me that the ball was in my court. The choice was mine. Once I was confronted with the truth, I had to choose.

41

When I did, empowered by his grace, my heart seized his words and the battle began. Confronted with words of faith that reflected God's reality, the enemy's grip on my heart and mind loosened and eventually released. The enemy could not maintain his hold when bombarded with words of truth. God's truth never comes unaccompanied. Its traveling companion is always freedom.

Spiritual warfare was a key component in the battle for my life. I'm not referring to spiritual hysterics, flamboyant deliverances, or verbal barrages flung at the enemy. I am referring to declaring God's word to be true in the face of circumstances that seem totally contrary to the declarations being made. The word of God is sharper than a two-edged sword piercing to the heart of the matter and dividing the pseudo-reality of the enemy from the actual reality of God. He invites us to live with and breathe in heaven's reality. Tell the enemy what God says. They are not simply wishful words of desperate people or magical incantations we hope will bring a change. They are powerful words of truth and freedom. *"They will stumble and fall...my heart will not be afraid...I will remain confident."*

It is imperative that we join God in the battle for our souls. I am not referring to the assurance of our salvation, which is found in and rests solely on Christ. I am referring to how we choose to live our lives as those who have been rescued by the love of God through the cross of Christ. Don't underestimate the potential of the declared word of God to put the enemy to flight. When we quote the word of God, we are not throwing empty words into the atmosphere. God's words contain an energy and authority that will change your heart, change your perspective regarding your circumstances, and often, though not always, change the circumstances themselves. The change may come immediately or it may come over a prolonged period of time. The appearance and timing of the outcome is in God's hands, but the tools and weapons to affect that outcome are very often in our own hands. We must put our hands to the plow of God's word and not look back. He will not fail us. Allow the word of God to seep deep into your being. If you do, when the wounds come, as they surely will, you will bleed the word and heart of God, and the enemy and his work will dissolve before the greatest force in the universe. Jesus said, *"The words I have spoken to you are spirit and life"* (John 6:63 NASB). As those spirit-lifed words flow from our heart and lips, the enemy will stumble and fall.

Chapter Five

What Do You Want The Most?

"The one thing I have asked of the Lord, the thing I seek the most is to live in the house of the Lord all the days of my life, delighting in the Lord's perfections and meditating in his temple."
Psalm 27:4

One of the most important things that has come out of my experience is a greater degree of and commitment to honesty. Honest with myself about myself, about my true feelings, the ones I'm actually experiencing rather than the ones I imagine I'm supposed to be feeling. Honest about my desires or my lack of them. Honest about what I really want or what I really do not want. Honest with others about the things it is important to be honest with others about; about relationships, about choices with long term consequences, about what matters the most. In Paul's letter to the Philippians, a church with which he had a very close relationship, he told them he wanted them to *"understand what really matters"* (Phil. 1:10). I can't imagine knowing something of more importance than *"what really matters."* It is a heritage I hope I'm able to leave my children and grandchildren.

What do you want the most? It's a question that must be, by everyone, seriously and thoughtfully answered, no matter what stage of life you are in. There is something each of us desires the most. I am not referring to anything as superficial as winning the lottery. I am referring to the vital issues of life, the things having to do with who we are and who we are becoming, things critical to the well-being of our hearts and the well-being of those around us. Becoming aware of our deepest desires is fundamental to understanding who we are, who God has made us. Parker Palmer states, "Before you tell your life what you intend to do with it, listen for what it intends to do with you."[10]

At various points in my life, the answer to the question of what I desired the most would have been different. In my childhood, I wanted my parents to live together. In my teen years, the thing I wanted the most was to be accepted by my peers. As a young man, I wanted to live long enough to get married and have sex. As the father of four boys, I wanted to be a good dad and my sons to grow up happy, healthy, and live lives filled with genuine meaning. Each of those desires says something about the person I was at that point in my life.

Depression robbed me of desiring anything meaningful. I reached a point where I didn't care about my future. I couldn't imagine I had one. To be truthful, I didn't care if I had one. Being honest about that, being able to admit I felt that way, actually proved to be a step in the right direction. At my lowest point, I became very aware how important it was that I should want *something*. The lack of desire was frightening. Not longing for anything is a sign you have lost touch with yourself. God reveals through the prophet Jeremiah that he has *a future and a hope* for us. He says that his plans for us *"are plans for good and not for disaster"* (Jer. 29:11).

Paul describes it in Philippians 3:13 as *"reaching forward to those things which are ahead."* We must be looking ahead. We must be forward-facing people. When we are not, there is a problem. Kierkegaard said, "Life can only be understood backward, but it must be lived forward."[11] The enemy desires to rob us of that future. He desires us to live in hopelessness and despair, the exact opposite of God's intention for our lives.

What do you want the most? It's not a question to be answered religiously. You can't mimic David's answer and imagine it to be true for yourself: *To live in the house of the Lord all the days of my life...delighting...meditating.* Is that what you really want or does it simply sound spiritual to say that you do? Those words uttered through some lips would be pompous and pharisaical, dripping with spiritual pride. Through others it would reflect a sincere desire, a statement that honestly reflects their hearts. Do I want something simply because someone else places a high value on it? Do I want something because I'm expected to want it? Or do I want it because I want it?

What I really wanted most was not to be depressed anymore. I wanted not to feel I was drowning in a sea of hopelessness and despair. What I wanted most was to be rescued from the emotional pit I had fallen into. That's what I really wanted. It wasn't spiritual. It wasn't sacrificial. It was as self-focused as it gets, but there is no doubt it is what I wanted the most.

I do believe David's declaration regarding his greatest desire warrants our reflection. However, I want to be clear this is *David's* desire. You cannot assume it is the thing you want the most at this point in your life. It is a lofty and noble desire and I have no doubt it truly reflected David's heart. It was a declaration I desired to be true of myself, but was in fact not true of my heart at that moment. David declared the thing he wanted the most was *"to live in the house of the Lord all the days of*

46

(his) life, delighting in the Lord's perfections and meditating in his temple."

Though these aspirations were not initially an honest reflection of my heart, as I lived with David's words I found meaning in them that wooed me away from the barren emotional place I was living. David asked of the Lord and diligently sought above all else that he might live in the house of the Lord all the days of his life. There is an historical context for this passage that mustn't be overlooked. The house of the Lord in David's time was a tent he had erected in Jerusalem within which the Ark of the Covenant, the tangible expression of God's presence, resided. It was the place above all places he desired to dwell. It was a few decades later that Solomon, his son, erected the temple that David first conceived and collected materials to build, a temple that provided physical rooms for priests to reside. Those were not available at the writing of David's psalm. Though David had a home of cedar, no doubt a home fit for a king, it was a tent in which he desired to live. Not just any tent to be sure. It was the dwelling of God on earth.

As a child I felt as if I lived at church. We were there every time the doors were open. In fact, we had a key so we could be there even when the doors weren't open. Unfortunately, much of society has grown up with the idea the local church building is God's house. Many have, thankfully, come to understand the fallacy of that belief and its unfortunate ramifications. It is no doubt a great blessing to have a facility in which a local church can gather. The question presents itself, then, how David's words apply to my life, if they apply at all. I did, in fact, discover a personal application, an application that surprised me. A desire, a deep desire, to live in the house of the Lord is a deep desire to live *in me*. This is proving to be a sobering thought. A desire to live, to dwell, where God lives, in God's house, is a desire to live with myself for I am now the dwelling of God. In a world in which many people are so very unhappy with themselves, David's desire as I have interpreted it could have a dynamic impact. To love God's house is to love ourselves, for we are, without a doubt, his house. The Bible is clear on this point. Jesus stated the second greatest commandment, surpassed only by loving God with all your heart, soul, and mind, is to love your neighbor *as you love yourself.* Loving yourself is not a foreign concept in Scripture; however, the reason I have just stated for loving yourself is something I had never considered. If I truly desire to adopt David's desire as my own, I will need to apply it in the day in which I live, in the only legitimate way it can be applied. I must desire above all things to live with the God who lives within me. I believe that will require a major paradigm shift in how many of us view ourselves. Rather than looking for ways to escape ourselves, we might need to begin looking for ways to live *with* ourselves and the God who lives in us.

God's word applied personally to me through this passage has had a substantial impact on how I view myself. It has not fostered pride; though that is a possibility I am certainly not above and am unfortunately quite susceptible to. I have encountered that particular flavor of pride in people who have flaunted and misapplied their perceived rights as the dwelling place of God. It has for me, instead, sparked a fresh sense of the incarnation, the word made flesh, living not just among us but in us. God incarnate, or, as Paul states it, the *"treasure in jars of clay"* (2 Cor. 4:7 NIV). Though the Incarnation has been orthodox theology for hundreds of years, it remains an astonishing thought, a thought we shall never fully understand this side of an eternity spent with that selfsame Word that became flesh. God has chosen to dwell in human flesh, my human flesh. A consuming desire to live with him in the place he has chosen to dwell is at the same time a consuming desire to live with me. To embrace this passage as I have represented it could prove to be a cure for self-loathing, self-pity, and low self-esteem among those acknowledging the indwelling presence of Christ. It could spark within us a confidence, which comes from living continually in God's presence, a confidence he always intended us to have. David's verse that immediately precedes the declaration of the thing he seeks most is, *"Even if I am attacked, I will remain confident"* (27:3). I believe that confidence comes from an abiding sense of God's presence, which can also prove to be a great antidote against the fear of the enemy. *"Though a mighty army surrounds me, my heart will not be afraid"* (Ps. 27:3).

There is no wrong answer to the question of what you seek the most, as long as the answer is an honest one. Whether what you want the most is what you need the most is another matter, but you must truthfully answer the first question or the second consideration is of no consequence because you are not living in personal honesty. Recently I saw a shopping mall map. They are posted at the main entrance of most malls, with an arrow or a star and the adjoining phrase *You Are Here*. That may be the most crucial discovery you'll ever make about yourself. Where are you? It's impossible to get where you think you want to go if you do not know where you are. Depression provided that for me. It put me on the map. It helped me determine my spiritual and emotional location. That singular discovery has returned me to the right path, headed for the future God has purposed for my life.

I'm still processing the question of what I want the most. David's response has certainly had a significant impact on me, but I am not assuming that his response is somehow now my response. I could throw out a pious declaration and represent it as my deepest desire and would no doubt elicit a chorus of amens, but I think it would be dishonest. For now, I think I'd rather continue to live in the question. Right answers aren't nearly as important to me as they used to be. Honest ones are.

49

Chapter 6

When Troubles Come

*"He will conceal me there when troubles come, he will hide me in his
sanctuary. He will place me out of reach on a high rock.
Then I will hold my head high above my enemies who surround me."*
Psalm 27:5-6a

Trouble had come. Life was a mess. I was a mess. I
had the facts to prove it. I had recited them often to those who
would listen, and many caring family members and friends did
listen. My report to them was a catalog of past woes updated
regularly with the most recent painful episodes. Those who
genuinely loved me wanted to know how I was doing. They
cared about me and about what was happening to me. They
patiently endured my list of grievances, most of them more
than once. God bless them for the grace they showed me.
Their love and friendship means more to me than I'll ever be

able to express. A subtle change, however, was happening within my soul. It wasn't a good one.

I noticed my conversations regarding my troubles began to feel rehearsed. When I spoke, I sounded like a lawyer arguing a case, against whom I wasn't sure. I found myself thoughtfully and intentionally organizing the information in hopes of a favorable verdict, from whom I'm not sure. The dawning recognition of what I was doing troubled me. Something was noticeably wrong, deeply wrong. It's not that I was inaccurately reporting my history. I had my facts straight. Facts, however, do not always portray the truth. They only do so if you have all the facts and fully understand the motives of those involved. Though we may think we possess the information required to make an accurate assessment, it's important we remind ourselves that in whatever circumstances we may be walking through only God has all the facts. He is the only one capable of a fair and unbiased conclusion.

Troubles come. They are inevitable. As mine came, I developed an unfortunate and unhealthy habit of adding them to a list I was keeping, which happens to be in direct contradiction to God's law of love. 1 Corinthians 13:5 clearly states that love *keeps no record of being wronged,* or, as another version rephrases, it *doesn't keep score of the sins of others* (TM). I felt wronged, robbed, and cheated. I was definitely keeping score and it was tilted decidedly in my opponent's favor.

Living in the dark prevents access to all the facts. My life seemed to revolve around the fact that *"troubles come."* It was all I could see. My field of vision had narrowed considerably through the years. Perhaps trouble was all my tunnel vision permitted me to see. Perhaps it was all I chose to see, which is a thought even more disturbing. The facts I was in possession of were killing me and they weren't doing much good for those around me. Something had to change. Thankfully, it did. The change began when the Lord, who is my light, began to shine on the words he had placed in David's heart so many hundred years ago.

"When troubles come" is such a small part of David's thought. The action of God in our behalf is what dominates the verse. *"He will conceal me...He will hide me...He will place me out of reach."* It is so typical of our humanity to focus on that which has to do with us as opposed to that which has to do with God. The verse states that he *will* act on our behalf, not that he *might* act on our behalf if we catch him on a good day. He *might* act on our behalf if we have been behaving according to his standards, have been good law abiding citizens, and have kept our noses clean. David unhesitatingly states that when troubles come he *will* act on our behalf.

What is it specifically David declares God will do? *"He will conceal me there when troubles come."* Where, specifically, is *there?* For that information, we must return to the previous verse. *"The one thing I have asked of the Lord, the thing I seek the most is to live in the house of the Lord all the days of my life, delighting in the Lord's perfections and meditating in his temple. He will conceal me **there** when troubles come."* There is the house of the Lord, the place David desires to live. One of the major points of the previous chapter is that I am the house of the Lord. If we carry that truth, as we should, into the current verse, the place in which the Lord wants to conceal me is within him...within me. Paul declares the same truth in his letter to the Colossians, *"Your real life is hidden with Christ in God"* (Col. 3:3). The place of concealment, of hiddenness, the place we are out of the enemy's reach is *hidden with Christ in God.* His place of abiding has already been established. By his choice, he has made his home within us. If we are looking for safety in some external, temporal setting we are wasting our time. If we believe we will find it in a special relationship with a valued friend, fellow Christian, or family member, our hope will fail. If we are expecting a practiced principle or daily discipline to provide the safety we so desperately seek, we will be sadly disappointed. The place of safety is within our own hearts, within the One who lives in our hearts. If we cannot find safety there, then it cannot be found and we will remain in jeopardy. It is a Person, not a practice or a place. Its sheltering walls are formed by relationship, not ritual. It is freely offered, not earned. Paul refers to it as *"the realities of heaven, where Christ sits in the place of honor at God's right hand"* (Col. 3:1). Paul's words bring us back to the point regarding whose reality we will choose to live in, God's or ours. Whose words are the truest? Whose motives are unquestionable? Who has promised to never leave or forsake us for any reason? Where will I choose to live? Within my perspective of the troubles that have come my way, or within the promised safety of the God who makes his home in me?

It's the same song, simply another verse. In my time of trouble I did not feel concealed, hidden in his sanctuary, or placed out of the enemy's reach. Does that mean it was not so? That is something each of us must decide for ourselves. Is God playing fast-and-loose with the truth, ignoring the reality of our circumstances and playing mind games with us? Is it all an illusion, like the woman in the magician's box who only appears to be sawn in two but who actually experiences no pain and miraculously escapes? My personal answers to those questions are *No* and *No*. God is incapable of operating in anything but truth. God is fully aware of our circumstances and our pain. He minimizes neither of them. His offer of safety is not sleight of hand, the illusive pea under the moving shells with only a desperate hope of picking the correct one.

In all fairness, though, what does that safety look like? In the case of David, it looked like his leader, the king, seeking to pin him against the wall with a spear. It looked like weeks of wandering in the Judean wilderness pursued by an army made up of his relatives. It looked like losing his best friend. On the other hand, it looked like victory in an apparently unwinnable fight against a seasoned giant warrior. It looked like the defeat of Israel's enemies in every battle in which David participated. It looked like deliverance from Saul on every occasion David was in jeopardy from him. Eventually, it took the form of the fulfillment of the word of God over David's life as he sat on the throne of Israel, ruling the people of God. I think we imagine safety to be a life of quiet ease secluded from the potential physical and relational dangers of this broken world. Hardly. The life of every biblical figure from Adam to Jesus says otherwise, not to mention the perils of Paul. Then what, in God's name, does safety mean?

It is soul safety. It is the thing I thought I had lost, but had not. It is the guarding of our essence, of the unique being we are. It is the safe keeping of our individuality, our identity, our personhood; in a word, our soul. The words of Christ say as much, *"Don't be afraid of those who want to kill your body; they cannot touch your soul. Fear only God, who can destroy both soul and body in hell"* (Matt. 10:28). *They cannot touch your soul.* Do we understand how powerful those words are? This may not appear to be a comforting word to those seeking relief from pain, grief, and despair, but I declare it is good news, the best news. The words I write now are not written to whitewash with a religious brush the genuine heartaches we face, attempting somehow to make them more palatable. My words are not an attempt to blunt the blow of the devastation of the AIDS epidemic in Africa, the famine of Sudan, or the genocide in Rwanda. I do write these words to unequivocally declare these earthly troubles and unimaginable travesties cannot rob us of who he has created us to be. There will be a day when *He will wipe every tear from (our) eyes, and there will be no more death or sorrow or crying or pain* (Rev. 21:4). I anxiously look forward to that day, but that day is not today. That fact does not mean we are less safe. God's promise of safety has to do with the soul and the promise of its preservation.

In 1944, at the age of fifty two, Corrie Ten Boom, and her sister Betsie were incarcerated by the Nazis for their role in the sheltering and protection of Jews during the Second World War. Corrie's father was imprisoned at Scheveningen and died ten days later. She and her sister experienced the horrors of Ravensbruck, the Nazi death camp in which Betsie lost her life. Corrie survived and documented this period of her life in her best-selling book *The Hiding Place*. If anyone knew what it was like for troubles to come, Corrie Ten Boom did. Despite her experiences she writes, "Happiness isn't something that depends on our surroundings...It's something we make inside ourselves."[12] She had found the place of safety, the heart of God within her own heart. She had been hidden in God's sanctuary. She had been placed on a high rock out of the enemy's reach. After the war, she returned to Holland and established houses of refuge for concentration camp survivors. Perhaps more amazingly she sheltered the jobless Dutch who previously collaborated with Germans during the occupation. She traveled the world for thirty years as an ambassador of the grace of God. Her message was always one of forgiveness. Corrie Ten Boom never lost her soul. "God's viewpoint is sometimes different from ours—so different that we could not even guess at it unless He had given us a Book which tells us such things....In the Bible I learn that God values us not for our strength or our brains but simply because He has made us."[13] *Simply because he has made us.* There is nothing more precious to God than who we are. He values us each uniquely. He has provided a sacred vault, an impregnable fortress, a safe place for our souls that none but he can access. It is his presence within us.

Try as they might, they could not touch Corrie Ten Boom's soul. In fact, her experience enriched and strengthened her. That which her enemies meant for evil, God turned for good and the forces of hell continue to pay the price as a result of the love she spread like a blanket across the world that had brought her trouble. Anger was deprived of its power and hatred denied its revenge. Grace and forgiveness reigned.

Darkness yielded to light because a spinster in Holland found safety in the refuge of the presence of God within her.

"Then I will hold my head high above my enemies who surround me." Throughout the psalm, David consistently acknowledges the ever present enemy; the evil one attempting to devour, the mighty army that surrounds. Nowhere is the existence of the enemy denied or ignored. On the contrary, he is regularly mentioned. We must possess a healthy awareness of the enemy. For the fearful, a consciousness of the enemy may cause them to cower. For the prideful, it often elicits a boastful barrage of rebukes, but for those who have found the safety of God's presence neither of those reactions occur. Instead, they lift their heads in the restful pose of confidence. Theirs is a posture of peace. Raised eyes view the remarkable vista God has laid out before the unobstructed gaze of their elevated position. Their heads are held high above their enemies, not in the arrogance of victory, nor in the gloating glare of the gladiator relishing the slaughter of his foe. They exhibit the unalarmed attitude of those who know they cannot be touched. They are out of reach. In another of his songs, David describes an additional posture that can be taken in the enemy's presence: *"You prepare a feast for me in the presence of my enemies"* (Ps. 23:5). In David's day, as in Christ's, meals were eaten while reclining at the table. In the middle of difficult circumstances and oppressing forces, we can hold our heads high or recline and enjoy a good meal. Both are appealing options. Corrie Ten Boom ate from this table. Her head held high in humility, she received from God's sumptuous supply and her soul grew fat. It must have been a source of great distress for her enemies.

We live with an ever-present enemy. This knowledge requires vigilance, not fear. We have the upper hand and must never believe otherwise. The enemy does not and will never have access to our souls as long we live in the place of safety that has been provided for us by our loving God. We can live the life of confidence and security our hearts crave. It comes as no surprise that the place of safety is within God. It may come as somewhat of a surprise that the place of safety is within God within *us*. I wholeheartedly agree that we, as followers of Christ, should live outwardly focused lives. We live in a world in desperate need of the God we know and love, but an outwardly focused life is dependent upon inwardly focusing on him. Then we will hold our heads high above our enemies who surround us. Then we will live in the safety and security that His presence provides.

Chapter 7

Singing Your Song

*"At his sanctuary, I will offer sacrifices with shouts of joy,
singing and praising the Lord with music."*
Psalm 27:6b

I have been involved with music for as long as I can remember. My mom and dad sang and played in a quartet with another couple in the church I grew up in. Both sets of parents involved the kids in aspects of the music. I remember my brother and I and the couple's three children singing a cutesy little song at a church music event when we were all really young. I hope that's not on video anywhere. I was mortified to be standing up in front of people singing. Despite the childhood embarrassment, however, music has always been a part of my relationship with God. For me, God and music have been synonymous terms. I understand that music and worship are not necessarily synonymous, but they have been for me. It's hard for me to imagine one without the other. The same seems to be true for David.

Here at mid-psalm David chooses to call attention to this, as if by his choice of placement in the psalm he is emphasizing its centrality in our lives. True worship is the adoration of God, the outpouring of our love for him. The moment we *use* worship (as if that is actually possible) as a vehicle to obtain something for ourselves it, at that moment, ceases to be worship. Nevertheless, in an atmosphere of true worship many things do happen in us and to us, including the ongoing healing of our hearts.

David was personally acquainted with the restorative power of the worship of God. He was not a stranger to the pit of despair. Yielding to the depravity of his own heart, he had committed terrible deeds in his life. On one occasion, he commissioned a murder to cover up his adulterous affair. His response of repentance regarding those deeds included the writing of a song. Though we no longer have the melody, here are some of the lyrics: *"Purify me from my sins, and I will be clean; wash me, and I will be whiter than snow. Oh, give me back my joy again; you have broken me—now let me rejoice. Do not banish me from your presence, and don't take your Holy Spirit from me...Forgive me for shedding blood, O God who saves; then I will joyfully sing of your forgiveness. Unseal my lips, O Lord, that my mouth may praise you... The sacrifice you desire is a broken spirit. You will not reject a broken and repentant heart, O God"* (Ps. 51:7-8, 11, 14-15, 17). In his most desperate moments, David turned to music to find his way back to God. The worship of God, especially as it is connected to music, is one of the most powerful activities we can involve ourselves in as we attempt, like David, to climb out of whatever pit we may have fallen in. Music touches something at the deepest levels of our lives physically, emotionally, psychologically, and spiritually, a fact that has now been scientifically verified.

A number of years back while browsing the web I came across something termed DNA music. In the recent past, scientists have learned how to map our DNA. The advances made in the field of human genetics are nothing less than astounding. The *Journal for American Medicine* states, "The year 2000 marked both the start of the new millennium and the announcement that the vast majority of the human genome had been sequenced."[14] One of the things discovered in this process is the fact that our DNA contains frequencies, the same frequencies it turns out, that are in music. We are literally *wired* for music. Strands of DNA have been decoded and converted into song. A quick search of the internet will yield a plethora of sources regarding the connection of DNA and music and companies that have been formed for the purpose of converting a strand of your DNA into song.[15]

My point does not relate to the scientific details, most of which I do not come close to understanding. Rather, it is the fact that music is apparently encoded at the molecular level of our being, at the deepest levels of biological life, in the fiber of who we are. In a word, each of us is a song. Because our DNA is as unique as a fingerprint, we are individually a one-of-a-kind song, a song no one else is capable of singing, and a song, if unsung, that cannot be replaced. The entire world suffers the loss when the refrain of our lives is not heard. Our living melody was destined to be joined with those of every other human being to form a magnificent song rising to God from every crevice of this planet. When we are not actively living out, for whatever reason, the person God has called us to be, we deprive the Father of one of the songs he has written. The cosmic symphony suffers because a harmony is missing.

Science is only beginning to understand the power of music. Music therapy has now become an accepted treatment in the medical community. "Music therapy is the use of music to promote, maintain and restore psychological, physical, emotional, and spiritual health. Music therapists use the power of music to connect with patients and families and provide outlets for expression of feelings, relaxation/stimulation, and communication."[16] A group of Turkish doctors in Istanbul have begun using music as a treatment for their patients at Memorial Hospital. "The *makam*, a musical mode unique to traditional Arabic and Turkish music, was used in Islamic medicine as early as the ninth century, when philosopher al-Farabi cataloged the effects of different musical modes on the human body and mind." The Turkish doctors have discovered that "...ten minutes of live music will lower a patient's heart rate and blood pressure without having to prescribe additional medicine."[17]

The power of music is not limited to the Christian faith just as DNA is not limited to the Christian faith. Music impacts all of humanity because all of humanity has been imbedded with music. The American Music Therapy Association lists the following benefits of music: "Brain function physically changes in response to music...It is often used to help rebuild physical patterning skills in rehabilitation clinics. Levels of endorphins, natural pain relievers, are increased while listening to music, and levels of stress hormones are decreased. This latter effect may partially explain the ability of music to improve immune function. A 1993 study at Michigan State University showed that even 15 minutes of exposure to music could increase interleukin-1 levels, a consequence which also heightens immunity...Research has proven that mothers require less pharmaceutical pain relief during labor if they make use of music."[18]

David, the singer/songwriter/musician understood music's power. He declares, *"Rise up, O Lord, in all your power. With music and singing we celebrate your mighty acts"* (Ps. 21:13). The power of God is somehow released in our musical celebration of God's presence. *"Sing praises to God, sing praises; sing praises to our King, sing praises! For God is the King over all the earth. Praise him with a psalm"* (Ps. 47:6-7). Singing is consistently connected to the King and his Kingdom and therefore to the act of reigning. David passed this knowledge and passion to his son, Solomon. When the temple was constructed, provision was made for singers and musicians to be constantly available for the worship of God (1 Chron. 6, 13, 15, 16). At one point, Solomon employed four thousand musicians solely for the worship of God.

I am acquainted with people who claim they have not a single musical bone in their body. In the past, I would not have argued the point with them. I have heard them sing and make attempts at playing musical instruments. You would be hard pressed to identify what came out of them as music. I have, however, changed my tune. With the mapping of our DNA and the discovery of its association with music, I would unequivocally state that they *do* have musical bones in their body; not just bones, but hair, fingers, and tendons that are full of music. Though they may not be gifted with an ability to express it in ways we would generally acknowledge as musically pleasing to our ears, their very being is filled with music.

Sadly, in my darkest times I could not find the strength or desire to practice what I preached. The loss of my soul was the loss of my song. There is a reason they call it soul music. Merriam-Webster defines soul music as being "characterized by intensity of feeling and earthiness."[19] I felt as if my soul had flat-lined. There was nothing coming from it but a dull hum. My life was simply white noise. Depression was the interruption of the song of my life. Psalm 137 was written at some point after the captivity of Israel. The conquered Jewish nation and its inhabitants had been transported to the land of the Babylonians. The writer of the psalm laments, *"By the waters of Babylon, there we sat down and wept, when we remembered Zion. On the willows there we hung up our lyres. For there our captors required of us songs, and our tormentors, mirth, saying, 'Sing us one of the songs of Zion!' How shall we sing the Lord's song in a foreign land?"* (Ps. 137:1-4 ESV). Indeed, how can we sing the Lord's song in a foreign land? Depression is a foreign land, a state of captivity. I was no longer residing in the home God had provided for me. I was a prisoner in a place I had no desire to be and with no prospect of escape. Survival became my goal. The thought of a prosperous soul had long since vanished. I sharpened my coping skills and hoped for the best. Though I had been a worship leader for years in churches, conferences, and small group settings across the US and abroad, I had no ability to sing the song of my life, the Lord's song, in a foreign land. Though I was still leading worship in corporate meetings, my soul was not singing. *"Offering sacrifices with shouts of joy"* was the farthest thing from my mind.

This was, thankfully, not the end of the story. God in his grace intervened for me in several ways. The gift of family and friends, those who love and care for you, is a crucial component in finding your way back to the light. These are people who have a shout to offer for you and over you when you are incapable of it yourself; the same people who have faith for you when you have none for yourself, who pray for you when you have no prayer for yourself, people who love you enough to do for you what you cannot do for yourself. I did have a responsibility in the matter. My responsibility was choosing to allow them to do that for me, to place myself in environments where the worship of God was occurring, to allow a song to be sung over me or a shout to be raised for me. One of the most destructive things you can do when you are in the condition I have described is to isolate yourself, to distance yourself from the very ones you should be spending time with. Do not permit the embarrassment you might feel as a result of the emotional state you find yourself in to keep you from the people you love and the people who love you. I attended gatherings I had no desire to go to because I knew I needed to be in the atmosphere of worship that would be present. The atmosphere of worship is fresh air for oxygen-deprived souls. God can and will breathe new life into us if we will choose to put ourselves in the midst of his worshipping people.

You can turn on a CD player, iPod, or stereo. You can immerse yourself in the abundance of authentic, heartfelt, God-breathed music that is available. You may not be able to utter a word, but you can listen. It's a choice, a choice only you can make, but you can make it. You will find it to be a life-giving choice. Just as family and friends are a remarkable gift from God, so is the voluminous amount of Spirit-inspired music we have at our disposal. Spirit-inspired music is not limited to the genre of Christian music. Some of the most reverential and God-honoring music ever written was created by a bevy of great classical composers. Bach, Beethoven, and Mozart, along with so many others, left us a legacy of divine melodies that have the power to revive the soul. God-music creates an atmosphere of healing within which we can rediscover our song. It can play a huge role in the recovery of the song of your life. In our darkness, the music stops. It's critical we use the music of others to help rekindle our own song.

When the prodigal son came to his senses and returned home, he received an unexpected surprise. A party in his honor. The elder son was not home when his younger brother made his return. It says of the older brother, *"As he came and drew near to the house, he heard music and dancing"* (Luke 15:25 ESV). Home is where the party is. Home is where the music is playing. Home is where you can recover you soul. Home is where your life can learn to sing again. Come home. There's a party waiting for the honored guest. There's a party waiting for you. *"At his sanctuary, I will offer sacrifices with shouts of joy, singing and praising the Lord with music."*

Chapter 8

Living with Doubt

"Hear me when I pray, O Lord. Be merciful and answer me.
My heart has heard you say, 'Come and talk with me,' and my heart
responds, 'I am coming.' Do not turn your back on me. Do not reject
your servant in anger. You have always been my helper.
Don't leave me now; don't abandon me, O God of my salvation!"
Psalm 27:7-9

      There is an air of uncertainty in these words that seems
totally at odds with those that precede them, statements
previously brimming with confidence in the Lord's care and
protection, assurances of a defeated foe, and David's promised
devotion and worship. His language now carries a sense of
unsure petition. He fears rejection and abandonment. Though
he acknowledges that God has previously come to his aid,
there is a noticeable desperation in his request that seems out
of place when compared to the previous tenor of his words.
Confidence has eroded into anxious concern. Faith in God's

ability has degenerated into fear of his anger. An assurance of God's presence is now an alarm of abandonment. What event has happened, what circumstance has changed that would cause such a shift in his tone? There is no indication in the psalm that anything has changed, but something has certainly shifted in his attitude. What has happened is that doubt has reared its ugly head and shaken David's heart.

Doubt: we all have it. There are moments it seems insurmountable. It threatens to derail our lives and casts a shadow over everything we thought we knew. At other times, it fades to the background and is hardly, if at all, noticed, but it is never gone. It is temporarily hiding. We will never completely be rid of it in this life, nor should we be. Why? Because doubt is the seedbed of faith. Experiencing doubt does not mean we have somehow surrendered the faith and are now in jeopardy of the fires of hell. Doubt is a permanent part of what it means to be human, an inescapable aspect of our existence. We ignore it at our own peril. We must deal with doubt. How we choose to deal with it will shape the course of our lives.

Though I had personally experienced the presence of God in powerful ways on many occasions, I entered a season in which doubt assaulted me on every front. On a good day, I could remember the sense of his presence and find some semblance of peace, some sense of relationship with God. On a bad day, I had trouble believing I had ever truly known God at all. When the bad days began to outnumber the good ones, I knew I was in trouble. Something was seriously wrong. I began looking for a way out, for the road back to the Father's house. I had somehow lost my way. I wasn't the first to experience this issue. According to the Bible, it is an experience common to all. No one, including Jesus himself, escapes unscathed. There is a way out, a way to harness the doubts we face and yoke them to the oxen of faith. First, however, the struggle must be acknowledged. That is what I hear David doing in the verses above.

This is not the only time David expresses his misgivings with pen and ink. He regularly admits his fears in writing. One of the consistent worries David faced was that God would somehow desert him. The same request occurs in a number of his songs. *"Do not stay silent. Do not abandon me now, O Lord"* (Ps. 35:22). *"And now, in my old age, don't set me aside. Don't abandon me when my strength is failing"* (Ps. 71:9). *"Don't abandon me, for you made me"* (Ps.138:8). Numerous passages reveal his fear of being forsaken by God and his earnest prayer that it not be so. Whether we understand why or not, David's concern regarding abandonment is, for him, a very real one. I do not believe he added these prayers for dramatic effect. How can we perceive his words as anything other than a genuine reflection of the condition of his heart? Possibly his most intense plea occurs in Psalm 22:1, *"My God, my God, why have you abandoned me? Why are you so far away when I groan for help?"* I regard it as the most intense of his prayers on this subject because these are the words found on the lips of Jesus as he hung on a Roman cross in the final minutes of his earthly life in an agony we cannot begin to comprehend (Matt. 27:46). There are those who believe Jesus was simply quoting scripture in order to bring messianic fulfillment to David's words. I believe that is misguided thinking and a weak attempt at masking the real humanity of Christ. I believe Jesus found in David's psalm words that expressed what he, himself, felt at that very moment: abandoned and forsaken. He used biblical language to give voice to his deepest anguish. According to the Gospels of Matthew and Mark, they are the last words he ever uttered as a pre-resurrection human being. *"My God, my God, why have you abandoned me?"*

The Scriptures are clear that Jesus experienced the gamut of human emotion. Those who have been presented an image of Christ that leaves no room for the experience of doubt, fear, or abandonment have been misled. *"We don't have a priest who is out of touch with our reality. He's been through weakness and testing, experienced it all—all but the sin"* (Heb. 4:15 TM). There is nothing we have felt that he did not feel. Our reality was his reality. As the King James Version states, he has been *touched with the feeling of our infirmities.* The Greek word for *infirmities* is most often translated as *weakness* and is used both of the body and the soul. It is used in the plural. It does not refer to an isolated, minor weakness but rather to the many weaknesses that are connected to being human. Jesus experienced it all, yet in all those experiences he did not sin.

Christ's fear and doubt regarding his ability to endure the Passion prompted his prayer for the cup of suffering, if possible, to be removed from him. It is difficult to imagine what he was feeling at that moment. In the end, he left the decision to his Father and accepted that decision and its consequences. Jesus' concern, like David's, was a real one, an experience so intense his physical body broke down under the stress. His soul was *crushed with grief to the point of death* (Matt. 26:38). He experienced betrayal at the hand of Judas and abandonment by his closest companions. Each of the remaining eleven disciples deserted him in the end. When the Roman nail was placed against his wrist and the hammer raised, is it not reasonable to believe he feared the pain he was about to experience? His fear, however, did not rule his actions. That does not mean he didn't experience it. Jesus clearly states he could have called a host of angels to deliver him. He did not allow fear to influence his decision to choose not to be rescued. Love overruled fear and he drank the cup of suffering his Father had given him. All we have ever felt, all we will ever feel, Jesus felt it long before us. Our feelings have touched his life. Yet, in it all, he did not sin. That is what sets him apart from the rest of humanity.

Jesus was not the only one to face and conquer his doubt. It would be difficult to make a case for anyone experiencing more loss than Job. The death of his children, financial catastrophe, the loss of his health, one tragic event after another, yet he cries out in the midst of his shattered life, *"Though he slay me, yet will I trust in him"* (Job 13:15 KJV). His choice to put his trust in God is courageous, but do you hear the uncertainty of his position? He had no assurance of deliverance, no promise of rescue from his devastating life circumstances. That is the very thing we are most often looking for: rescue, assurance of deliverance. Aren't those the things that indicate we are loved by God? And if we do not receive them our world is rocked, God has forsaken us, and it appears serving him is futile. The preacher of Ecclesiastes calls it *"vanity of vanities"* (NKJV) or as *The Message* phrases it, *"Smoke, nothing but smoke."* Job's choice to trust did not rest on the absence of doubt or the assurance of deliverance but rather his confidence in God.

The three young Hebrew men subjected to the fires of Nebuchadnezzar's furnace made a similar choice. *"The God whom we serve is able to save us...But even if he doesn't, we want to make it clear to you, Your Majesty, that we will never serve your gods or worship the gold statue you have set up"* (Dan. 3:17-18). They were not arrogantly prophesying their coming deliverance. The certainty of their physical wellbeing was far from settled. In fact, they declared unequivocally their deliverance was not a foregone conclusion. Their choice to place their trust in God was, as Job's, made in the midst of a doubtful outcome, but there was nothing doubtful about their choice.

The fact I have experienced doubt in my own personal life is not an issue. The issue is that I sinned in my doubt. In my doubt, I failed to trust. Trust is not the absence of doubt. In fact, trust cannot occur outside the arena of doubt. Doubt must be present for trust to manifest. Paul Tillich states, "Doubt isn't the opposite of faith; it is an element of faith."[20] That is a shocking thought to many. Doubt is a required ingredient of faith and trust. Paul states in his letter to the Romans that *"everything that does not come from faith is sin"* (14:23 NIV). Some have interpreted that passage to mean that doubt is sin. Experiencing doubt is not sin. Refusing to allow faith to be birthed out of doubt is sin. It is the very reason for the statements David wedges in between his declarations of doubt. *"Do not turn your back on me. Do not reject your servant in anger. **You have always been my helper.** Don't leave me now; don't abandon me, **O God of my salvation!**"* Though David allows his doubts to surface, he allows faith to emerge as well. Listen to the words of the psalmist at other moments in his life. *"I love the Lord because he hears my voice and my prayer for mercy"* (Ps. 116:1). *"The Lord will answer when I call to him"* (Ps. 4:3). *"I am praying to you because I know you will answer, O God"* (Ps. 17:6). If David knows that God hears his voice, if he is assured of an answer, why desperately request that he be heard by God? Because David, like you and I, lived with doubt. At moments, we struggle with what we are facing and in our weakness doubts arise. It is a much greater mistake to internalize doubt than it is to express it. Internalized doubt is the seedbed for resentment, anger, and bitterness. Doubt that is honestly acknowledged has the potential of being the seedbed of faith. You may wish it was otherwise, that we can and would in this life attain a place of faith in which doubt was squeezed from our being never again to plague us. It is a false, but understandably appealing, wish.

What is true of faith is true, as well, of hope. *"Now hope that is seen is not hope. For who hopes for what he sees? But if we hope for what we do not see, we wait for it with patience"* (Rom 8:25 ESV). In the same way that the absence of the object of hope is the reason hope exists, the presence of doubt is the reason faith exists. Experiencing doubt or hopelessness is not the end of the world. In fact, if we permit it, it can be the beginning of a brand new world. The same doubting David also wrote these words, *"When doubts filled my mind, your comfort gave me renewed hope and cheer"* (Ps. 94:19). God will provide for us the same comfort, hope, and cheer that he provided David. David found it to be so. Jesus found it to be so. We will find it to be so.

Paul's description of what he faced rings true in my heart. *"We are hard pressed on every side, but not crushed; perplexed, but not in despair; persecuted, but not abandoned; struck down, but not destroyed"* (2 Cor. 4:8-9 NIV). Paul made a choice in the face of difficult circumstances, circumstances certainly severe enough for doubt to gain the upper hand and turn the tide of battle against him. He made a choice to view his circumstances from another perspective. Not crushed, not in despair, not abandoned, and not destroyed. He found a way to harness his doubts to the oxen of faith and continue to plow the field he had been given to work in, to finish the race he had been given to run, to stand his ground until the final punch had been thrown, and to receive the prize which had been set aside for him. Doubt that is harnessed to faith is a lethal combination. It deals a death blow to the work of the enemy. We have taken what he meant for evil (i.e., doubt) and have turned it into a powerful weapon for good, faith. We must adopt a new perspective regarding our doubts. We must allow them to be launching points for kingdom advance, not obstacles that stop us dead in our tracks.

"Hear me when I pray, O Lord. Be merciful and answer me." I want to live a life of prayerful expectation, not prayerful resignation. Dutiful prayer is not a prayer that expects an answer. I'm pretty sure it pleases God that I pray, so I pray. This was a point of honesty I came to in my own life, a doubt I had to face. I am praying. I am praying because I'm supposed to pray. I am praying because I think it pleases God if I pray, but I am praying with no expectation of an answer. James declares in his epistle, *"People who 'worry their prayers' are like wind-whipped waves"* (James 1:6 TM). What a remarkable rendering of that verse by Eugene Peterson. *"People who 'worry*

their prayers'..." I have no desire to *worry my prayers* and I am positive God has no desire to hear them. I am coming to grips with the fact that doubt is and will always be a part of my life. I am committed to allowing my doubts to become fertile ground for faith. I take great comfort from Jude's admonition, *"Be merciful to those who doubt"* (Jude 1:22). For Peter, the only one of the twelve who responded to Jesus' invitation to get out of the boat (Matt. 14:31), to doubt was to sink, but the hand of Jesus was immediately extended to him. There is mercy for those who doubt. It is a mercy that is new every morning.

David prayed for God to answer him and then immediately records for us the answer he received. I love the answer. God's answer to David's request to be heard was, *"Come and talk with me."* The solution to our problem, the light for our darkness, the answer to our question, the satisfaction of our deepest need is always the same. It always has been. It always will be. It is what we have been created for. We cannot exist in any real sense of the meaning of existence without it. It comes as an invitation, *"Come and talk with me."* Communion with God: Father, Son, and Holy Spirit. Nothing takes the place of it. Nothing suffices. Life is found in no other place. David's salvation was found in the fact that when God beckoned him to come, he came. In all his weakness, failure, doubt, and fear he came. When called, he came. He gave no elaborate arguments regarding his unworthiness. He made no excuse for his many sins and his checkered past. When called, he came. That is why he is known as a man after God's own heart. Out of that place of communion was born the heart of a warrior, the heart of a worshipper, the man with a desire to build a house for God so he could live among his people. Though he did not ultimately build it, he made preparation for that house and passed the task to his son, but David's fingerprints were all over it. Why? Because when God called, he came.

One of the greatest contributing factors to my slide into a pit of despair was the fact that I quit coming. It wasn't that I never came. It was that more and more often duties and details became more important than coming. I could come later, when I was through with my tasks. My time with God would be better then, I reasoned. My mind and heart would be less distracted after I had cleared a few things off my plate, but somehow my plate never got cleared and I never came, at least not very often, certainly not often enough. It is the thing I regret the most. It is the thing that has most dramatically changed regarding how I choose to live my life now. I come. Before anything else, I come. Without being called I come, for I understand I have a standing invitation. *"Come and talk with me"* and my heart responds, *"I am coming."* I understand David's desperate cry in the middle of his song. It was the cry of my own heart. *Hear me! Have Mercy! Don't leave me! Answer me!* And he did. The answer I received was the answer David received. *"Come and talk with me."* By his grace, my response will continue to be *"I am coming."*

Chapter 9

Always There

"Even if my father and mother abandon me,
the Lord will hold me close."
Psalm 27:10

My parents divorced when I was six years old. It was the first of their divorces. They were remarried seven years later. Their second marriage lasted for a year. My brother and I lived with my mom following the first divorce and spent weekends with my dad. Following their second divorce we lived with my dad. My mom and dad both had multiple marriages to other spouses over the next number of years. I lost count after a while. I also ceased caring. My mom moved out of state and I saw her sporadically. She was absent for most of my junior high and all of my senior high years. As a child of divorce, you cope the best you can. Our emotional survival skills are quite remarkable. No one, however, avoids the negative emotional damage of a broken home.

Children are the natural result of the union of a man and a woman. There is a reason for that. The ideal environment for each child born into this world is to be raised in a home in which a man and a woman, a father and mother, are present. We are regrettably very far from that ideal. As a result, the emotional suffering of children in our world is nothing short of catastrophic. It is not news that the traditional family unit is no longer traditional. Currently, fifty percent of marriages in the United States end in divorce. It is not restricted simply to the young who have foolishly chosen a spouse in haste or acted on lustful impulses. In Canada, the age group with the highest divorce rate is those fifty-five to fifty-nine years old. More than one fourth of children under the age of eighteen now live in a single parent home. Whether intended or not, a sense of abandonment by a child of divorce is almost inescapable. The older the child at the time of the divorce, the more understanding they may have regarding the reasons for the divorce, but separation from a parent has major emotional ramifications.

According to the National Abortion Federation, "Each year, almost half of all pregnancies among American women are unintended. About half of these unplanned pregnancies, 1.3 million each year, are ended by abortion."[21] Since the legalization of abortion in 1973, more than fifty million have been performed in the United States. Abortion is, perhaps, the ultimate expression of parental abandonment. It is without a doubt the most permanent.

Intentionally or unintentionally, the abandonment of a child in our society occurs at an alarming rate: divorce, the death of a parent, a physically present but emotionally absent parent, abortion, neglect, abuse. The causes are numerous. The thing David mentions as his worst nightmare occurs on a regular basis in our broken world. UNICEF presently estimates the number of orphans across the world at 210 million. *"Even if my father and mother abandon me..."* has become a worldwide brutal reality.

As far as I know, we have no biblical or historical record that David's father or mother ever abandoned him. For that reason, David's inclusion of this verse seems a bit odd to me. Perhaps it is simply a metaphor, the worst kind of earthly abandonment he could imagine. In the world in which David lived, family was everything. Family loyalty was sacrosanct. The authority that the head of the household exercised was unquestioned. Elderly parents, generally speaking, were valued for their wisdom and counsel. The fifth commandment given to the children of Israel at the foot of Mount Sinai had to do with the honoring of fathers and mothers. In Ephesians 6, Paul notes that the fifth commandment was the first, if obeyed, to which a promise was attached, that of long life. Paul goes on to admonish fathers not to *"provoke your children to anger by the way you treat them. Rather, bring them up with the discipline and instruction that comes from the Lord."* The decision of a parent to abandon a child is completely foreign to the heart of God. It was, for David, the man after God's heart, the worst thing he could imagine happening to himself.

This particular passage from David's song has had a very personal impact upon me. For the sake of context, the verse needs to be heard in connection with the previous one. *"Don't leave me now. Don't abandon me, O God of my salvation. Even if my father and mother abandon me, the Lord will hold me close."* It is the continuation of David's earnest plea not to be abandoned, not to be left by God. In David's inimitable way, he voices his fear and then comforts himself with the truth. His fear that God would abandon him is addressed to the God he describes as his salvation. He then states what must have been for him the most unthinkable and frightening circumstance: *Even if my father and mother abandon me...*

There have, of course, been dysfunctional families making their home on this planet since Adam and Eve's regrettable decision to seek godhood. Lot, the nephew of Abraham, and his two daughters fled to the mountains for safety and lived in isolation following the destruction of Sodom and Gomorrah, communities famous for their perverse behavior. In fear of living out the remainder of their lives childless, the girls designed a plan that included the deliberate inebriation of their father and, on successive nights, having sexual intercourse with him while he was passed out drunk. The pregnancies resulted in the birth of Moab and Ammon whose descendants became lifelong enemies of God's chosen family, Israel. Isaac's fondness for Esau and Rebekah's for Jacob set in motion a deceitful plan that resulted in Jacob fleeing for fear of his life and the resulting separation of the family for twenty years. Though the family was reunited, the descendants of Esau, Jacob's brother, became lifelong adversaries of Jacob's family, the eventual family line of Christ. David's own family was certainly not immune to serious problems. One of his sons raped his sister. She lived in shame for the remainder of her life and the offending son fled to another country. Family jealousy, envy, hatred, and offense have devastating results. Much, if not most, of the responsibility for those results must land in the laps of parents. Endless biblical examples could be cited of careless and unloving parenting and the resulting family disintegration. Exodus 34:7 speaks of *the sins of the parents* and the effect it has *upon their children and grandchildren* until *the entire family is affected.*

"Even if my father and my mother abandon me..." In my darker days, I distinctly remember the first time I read this verse, really read it. I was immediately transported back to an early childhood memory, standing in the carport door with my mom and brother as my dad left for the first time. It is the root that eventually grew into a tree of painful experiences. It was no one's intention. Nevertheless, it was the consequence. When I was old enough to develop some hindsight, to

understand something of what had happened, I passed my share of blame around to those I believed it was owed. Like a deck of cards, I dealt them the hand I thought they deserved. I never did it verbally. I was much too timid for that. It was an internal activity. That particular approach to dealing with pain is worthless. First, the fact that it remains internalized simply exacerbates the problem. Secondly, you never have all the facts and your judgment is deeply flawed regarding who might be to blame. It simply further clouded the blurred lens through which I saw and interpreted my life. I had a log in my eye that needed removing before I would ever be capable of helping anyone else with whatever splinter might be affecting their own vision.

I had the opportunity to spend three days with a friend of mine who is especially gifted in the area of inner healing prayer. I had never experienced inner healing of anything up to that time. For the most part, I believed that type of prayer probably had benefited some people. I had no reference point for what that might look or feel like. I had very muted hopes of anything actually happening. My situation, however, was desperate. I was more than willing to explore the healing of my heart through this particular type of prayer despite my low expectations. In our first session, the childhood memory of my family in the carport was the first one we explored. I will never forget the experience. It, and the following days of prayer, changed my life forever.

Referring to what happens in inner healing as prayer is, for me, a bit of a misnomer. The person leading the session facilitates a time in which you and Jesus interact regarding the events that have been the source of great pain in your life. One of my reservations regarding this type of ministry was the thought of *seeing* Jesus in the memory, as though I had to somehow insert him in my past experience. My perspective regarding that totally changed when I realized one simple and rather obvious fact: he had been there all the time. He has always been with me. He is with me now. He was with me when I was six. I did not need to insert him in the memory. I simply needed to see him, for he had been there with me.

As we visited that moment in my early life in the carport of my childhood home, I was quite honestly shocked at how quickly I saw him. When I say I saw him I mean I saw him in my mind's eye in the place where memories exist, the place from which you can recall them and revisit them. You can often recall specifics of a memory in detail because they have become a part of you. I saw him, Jesus. He was standing off to the side, watching intently what was going on. Though I was standing with my mom and brother, I was also standing with him. He was holding my hand. I was describing this scene to the person leading me in this prayer time. She asked Jesus if there was anything he wanted to say to me. I distinctly heard him say in my heart, "You don't have to do it anymore." "Do what?" I replied. "You don't have to protect yourself anymore. I will." The chapter entitled "The Magic Button" is a result of that conversation. Though the memory concerned something that happened more than a half century earlier, the truth I was being given was for the present. I didn't have to protect myself anymore, *now*. He was my fortress *now*, my protector from danger *now*. It was a truth that would radically change how I would live my life in the present. I could quit pushing the button, lower the wall, and trust my Friend and my Savior with the protection of my heart.

It's difficult to put into words what happened. Christ's words to his disciples as recorded in John 8 about knowing the truth and the truth making you free probably comes closest to describing it. Something changed inside of me. I sensed a freedom I had never experienced. Fear and pain seemed to simultaneously vanish. Anxiety dissipated into thin air like wisps of smoke from a dying campfire. The scene shifted and I was now standing with my mother and brother. As I described that to my counselor, she asked if I sensed any pain in my heart. No. I could detect no pain. She asked me if I thought I could reach out and take Jesus' hand and walk off from that memory. Yes, I thought I could and that I should. So I did. I walked away from that place. I still possess within me that fifty-two-year-old memory in the place where memories live, but now there is no pain associated with it. It has become part of my past that I have possessed. It no longer possesses me. There is a world of difference between those two things.

One more notable thing happened before we left the memory. My counselor asked Jesus if there was anything else he wanted me to know. As a matter of fact, there was. He told me on that night, the night my parents separated, they abandoned me. Not in a physical sense. I lived with both of them either together or, after divorces, with each of them individually, until my senior year of high school at which time I moved in with my paternal grandparents. I was not physically abandoned that night, but I was emotionally abandoned. I don't blame them for that. At the same time, I do not excuse them for their actions. They answer to God for their decisions, not to me. They were both in such pain they simply did not have room for me. I don't mean to imply they didn't love me. They did. They were, however, incapable of being there for me, but Jesus was. Though I was not able at that moment to avail myself of his comfort and love, he was there. He always had been there. He always will be there. He is incapable of not being there. He can't help himself. He is Immanuel, God With Us.

Once upon a time, on a very dark night, in the middle of a very rough sea, Jesus and his companions were crossing Lake Galilee. Jesus was sleeping. His disciples were frantic. They woke him from his sleep. If they hadn't, he would have slept through the storm all the way to the other side of the lake. He obviously knew something they did not. Though there was a very real storm, there was no real danger. He was safe and would remain so, and consequently so would they. He slept because he knew this. They did not sleep because they didn't know this. I am convinced, though, that the truth is there to be known by us all. That does not diminish the reality of the storm, but it radically changes our perspective in the storm. In a panic, they woke him. They were sure they were going to drown. Jesus responded, *"Why are you so afraid?"* He said a similar thing to water-walking Peter as he began to sink, *"Why did you doubt?"* Jesus knew. He always knew. He was there. He will always be there.

The promise of Hebrews is a real one: *"For God has said, 'I will never fail you. I will never abandon you'"* (Hebrews 13:5), or as the Amplified Version records it, *"For He [God] Himself has said, 'I will not in any way fail you nor give you up nor leave you without support. [I will] not, [I will] not, [I will] not in any degree leave you helpless nor forsake nor let [you] down (relax My hold on you)! [Assuredly not!].'"* God will never abandon us. Assuredly not!

I think my favorite version of Psalm 27:10 comes from the English Standard Version. *"For my father and my mother have forsaken me, but the Lord will take me in."* Fifty-two years after the fact, the Lord took me in. He was there all along. He had never been absent, but on a Tuesday morning a half century after the fact, the Lord took me in and my life changed forever. My heart was healing. My eyes were opening. My darkness was dissipating. My depression was lifting. The Lord had taken me in.

Chapter 10

To Live Again

"Teach me how to live, O Lord.
Lead me along the right path,
for my enemies are waiting for me.
Do not let me fall into their hands.
For they accuse me of things I've never done;
with every breath they threaten me with violence."
Psalm 27:11-12

Living is a tricky business. You might imagine it simply to be a matter of breathing in and out, retaining a heartbeat, and a few other vital bodily functions. In a sense, you would be correct. We would describe a person functioning like that as alive, yet it is a far cry from living. My mom is currently in a nursing home. She has been for several years. She suffers severely from Alzheimer's disease. She is completely immobile. She no longer knows who we are and speaks in something they call *word salad* which is a conglomeration of words thrown together in no coherent order. We still visit her. Not as often as we used to. It's very difficult to see her in that condition and, at least as far as we can tell, no meaningful interaction takes place. But we still go. I wouldn't describe what my mom is doing as living.

I wonder what prompted David to pray the prayer he prayed? *"Teach me how to live again, O Lord."* Had he forgotten how? Had circumstances robbed him of the ability to live a life of meaning and purpose? Had betrayal, accusation, and violence drained him of his vitality for living? Had the threats of the enemy worn down his resolve and his trust eventually given way to fear? We were created by God to live, to really *live*. We've been designed for more than existence. Really living can and does have many expressions, but chief among them must surely be a deep and abiding sense of joy. Teilhard de Chardin said, "Joy is the infallible sign of the presence of God."[22] It's how you know he is around. I'm not referring to hilarity or anything as fleeting and unstable as a sense of happiness, as enjoyable as that might be. I am talking about a foundation stone of joy laid deep in your life that is not affected by a change in the emotional or physical atmosphere that occurs in or around you. In the midst of rebuilding Jerusalem's wall from the rubble of the enemy's destruction, Nehemiah declared *"the joy of the Lord is your strength"* (Neh. 8:10). The converse would be: no joy, no strength. I have personally found that to be true. I am not intending to imply that life is one big party and pain and suffering are a thing of the past once you have God in your life. They are, in fact, an inescapable part of life. I am saying that God is a God of joy and he created life to be enjoyed.

The most definitive sign that I was severely depressed was the fact I didn't enjoy anything anymore. Nothing. Nada. Zip. My passion had lost its punk. My conversations were contrived. Relationships were wearying. My hobbies were hobbled. As Ernest Lawrence Thayer wrote in his famous poem about the vagaries of baseball, "There is no joy in Mudville—mighty Casey has struck out."[23] That perfectly describes how I felt. I had struck out. I went down swinging, for sure, but the game was irrecoverably lost and sadness ruled the day. There was no discernible joy I could detect in any area of my life. Initially, it was my little secret, for I acted like I enjoyed a few things. That, however, was just for appearance sake. I still laughed at times. The laugh was real in the sense that I was actually laughing, but it wasn't genuine. It was something I used to cope. Proverbs states that a merry heart can do you good like a medicine. This wasn't a merry heart. It was a cheap substitute, a designer knock off from a foreign country. It wasn't a medicine, but a drug I was abusing. I laughed to distract myself from how I was feeling, much like a heroin addict would shoot up or an alcoholic take a drink. I used it to try and feel other than I was feeling. It didn't work. Recreational drugs are lousy substitutes for the real thing, for true joy.

I followed a reality TV show for a while, *Mountain Men*, that documented the lives of three men and their families who were living off the land, one in the wilds of Alaska, one in the mountains of Montana, and the other in the hills of North Carolina. On one particular episode they interviewed the fellow from North Carolina. The question was put to him, "What do you do for a living?" I thought his answer was intriguing. "I live for a living." His words were like a dart flung at me. I had forgotten how to live, to take life as it comes, as God brings it to us. The moments of our lives occur one right after the other. They don't ask our permission to happen. They just happen. They are the proverbial river into which you can never insert your foot in the same place twice. Every moment the river is a new one. Nothing stays the same. *Is* turns into *was* before you can blink your eye. Life was passing me by and I was missing out.

The road out of my blackness involved a number of things. It's difficult to say what was most important because all of it was essential. There is no doubt, however, that praying the prayers of David from this twenty-seventh psalm was one of the most significant things I did. This particular prayer passed my lips more times than I can count. *Teach me how to live, O Lord.* I was no longer living. I survived the best I knew how from one day to the next, but I was not living. I existed. I breathed in and out. I knew I was alive because my heart still hurt. I didn't know what else to do, so I offered up the prayer over and over. *Teach me how to live again, O Lord.* And he did.

How did it happen? There were steps toward healing, no doubt, but I have resisted the urge to categorize, analyze, and produce a nice little list to follow so you, too, can experience this amazing healing! Proposing a tidy remedy puts me in the mind of a snake oil salesman, or one of those gentlemen on the infomercials selling you the last knife you'll ever need in the kitchen. One size does not fit all. I believe the components that were put in place in my life were vital. Your road to recovery may very well include every one of them; then again, perhaps not. In the end, encountering the love of God is what will heal you. I encountered his love through his word, through the prayers of those who loved me, through books I read and songs I listened to, but in the end they were only channels for God's amazing love. Only his love can teach you how to live again.

Immediately after my time of inner healing prayer, I spent a week at a beautiful ranch situated on the edge of the Texas hill country. It is owned by some friends who graciously extended their hospitality to me for a time of rest and recovery. On my second day at the ranch, I took a long, rambling walk across their three hundred and twenty acres of rolling Texas countryside. At some point during the walk, I unexpectedly laughed out loud. It shocked me. I stopped dead in my tracks. The laugh had escaped all on its own. It wasn't premeditated. It wasn't for the benefit of anyone around me. It wasn't a drug. It spontaneously erupted from somewhere deep within. I stood there among the oak trees considering what had just happened. They have green oak and post oak on the ranch. The green oaks retain their leaves all year long. In the fall, the post oaks transition into beautiful reds and yellows and then shed their entire canopy. They were in the process of doing just that. At some point on my walk, I jumped a pair of doe a few hundred feet in front of me and watched them bound away, their white tails disappearing into the distance. I laughed again. Out loud. I couldn't seem to help myself. The beauty of the moment and the place seemed more than I could stand. So I laughed. As I did, I felt the healing medicine of a joyful heart begin to permeate my soul. It had been so long since anything like that had happened to me. At some point, it dawned on me. God was answering my prayer. I was learning how to live again. David prayed to the Lord in Psalm 13, *"Restore the sparkle to my eyes, or I will die"* (13:3). I could feel my eyes beginning to sparkle again.

This experience was only the first. It happened regularly over the remainder of my time at the ranch. Belly laughing at a friend's tale of an embarrassing moment, feeling deep pleasure as a four-hundred-pound steer ate cow feed out of my hand, gazing awestruck at a Texas sunset while sitting on the porch one evening, watching in wonder as nine doe and yearlings came early one morning to feed by the pond in front of the house. God had healed and was continuing to heal my heart. I was learning how to live again.

Lead Me Along The Right Path

Right paths have always been important to me, but probably for some wrong reasons. This was my version of a right path. 1) I don't want to get it wrong. I don't like getting it wrong. It makes me feel bad to get it wrong, so tell me what the right path is because I don't want to be wrong. 2) What are the rules? I like knowing the rules. There's some sort of sick safety in knowing and keeping the rules. I like that sick safe feeling I get thinking I kept the rules, believing I did it right. So tell me the rules. 3) Show me the right path. I like knowing where I'm going. Right paths lead to right places. Arriving at correct destinations is important, so show me the right path so I can wind up in the right place having gotten there the right way.

Sick, I know, but it felt safe and feeling safe was a high priority. My thinking wasn't as premeditated as I just described, but in hindsight all I described is true. I was the kid who always knew the memory verse in the Bible competitions in Sunday School because it was the right thing to do. I never got detention in public school. Like Paul the Pharisee, when it came to the Law I was blameless. Seat belts on, speed limits observed (at least most of the time). No trouble with the authorities. In fact, no trouble with anyone. I was just trying to get it all right. I somehow felt getting it right was going to be my salvation.

Don't get me wrong, there is a right path. David's prayer is that God will show him that path. The path, however, might be other than what we think it is. It turns out it is about much more than maps and boundaries and rules. I am learning that the trip itself is much more important than arriving, the act of journeying more valuable than the destination. In my focus on the right path, I was missing out on the life to be lived while traveling the path. It turns out there are fellow travelers. This is not something I am doing alone, but in the community and presence of others. It turns out that arriving in what I considered to be a timely manner is not all that important. The time I spend with my companions along the way is. It's not solely about the going, but rather going together. It's the daily walk and the people you are walking with that matter. It is learning to live in the moment, to be present to God, to yourself, and to others. This concept of approaching life as a journey is not a new one. People have advocated it for hundreds of years. It was not a new idea even for me. In my study of early Celtic Christian spirituality, it was one of the things I admired most about the way they lived their lives. I simply wasn't healed enough to live that way. The best I could do was talk about living that way. But things have changed. He's answering my prayer. He's teaching me how to live. He's showing me the right path.

For My Enemies Are Waiting For Me

They seem to crop up everywhere in this psalm. Enemies. They simply won't go away. False accusations, threats of violence. David says in another place, *"Many enemies try to destroy me, demanding that I give back what I didn't steal"* (69:4). Enemies don't play fair. They never will. Peter describes Satan as a roaring lion prowling around looking for someone to devour (1 Pet. 5:8). Following the rejection of Cain's offering, God had these words for him, *"But if you do not do what is right, sin is crouching at your door"* (Gen. 4:7 NIV). Right paths are important. We stray from them at our own risk. The depiction of sin as *"crouching at the door"* sounds so similar to David's description of the enemy in this song. They *"are waiting for me."* In another of David's psalms he describes them as *"those who lie in wait for my soul"* (Ps. 59:3). We need not live in fear, but we best not live in ignorance. David's repeated reference to the enemy in Psalm 27 is not a mistake. We have a real enemy who has real designs on the destruction of our lives.

It wouldn't be wisdom to imagine that we will ever be rid of our enemies. Until the final judgment, they will always be present. Dietrich Bonhoeffer knew something of living among his enemies. He served Christ as a Lutheran minister in the darkest days of Hitler's reign in Germany. His words are worth noting. "It is not simply to be taken for granted that the Christian has the privilege of living among other Christians. Christ lived in the midst of his enemies. At the end all his disciples deserted him. On the Cross he was utterly alone, surrounded by evildoers and mockers. For this cause he had come, to bring peace to the enemies of God. So the Christian, too, belongs not in the seclusion of a cloistered life but in the thick of foes. There is his commission, his work." Bonhoeffer then quotes these words from Martin Luther, "The Kingdom is to be in the midst of your enemies. And he who will not suffer this does not want to be of the Kingdom of Christ; he wants to be among friends, to sit among roses and lilies, not with the bad people but the devout people. O you blasphemers and betrayers of Christ! If Christ had done what you are doing who would ever have been spared?"[24]

Though our enemies will remain ever present, there is a safe path among them. It is the right path David was asking God to lead him along. Consider these verses from Isaiah 35: *There will be a highway called the Holy Road* (TM). *Evil minded people will never travel on it. It will be only for those who walk in God's ways* (NLT). *It's...impossible to get lost on this road* (TM). *Lions will not lurk along its course, nor any other ferocious beasts. There will be no other dangers. Only the redeemed will walk on it* (NLT). A road on which, if you remain, the enemy has no access to you. There is no danger on this road. Evil minded people can't travel it. Stay on the road and it's impossible to get lost.

This is not a road to a destination. It's a way of life, a way of living. It includes many of the things that I have referenced in previous chapters. A commitment to live in the light, to allow God to be your protector, choosing to believe and voice God's reality over what you believe to be your reality, a choice to worship God with songs of praise and heart melodies, a decision to be honest with yourself and with God about yourself and your feelings. It is all these things and more. It is the road we are called to walk, the right path to walk. God can and will show us the path, but in the end we must choose to stay on it. If we do, though the enemy may be waiting for us, he will have no access. He cannot come on this path.

If you read the thirty-fifth chapter of Isaiah, you will discover the path, the one the enemy has no access to, is a desert road. That may not initially seem very appealing, however if you continue to read, an amazing thing occurs. The desert is transformed as you walk this road. It becomes a place where flowers bloom, a place of rivers, streams, and pools of water. It becomes a place full of singing and joy. It becomes *as green as the mountains of Lebanon. There the Lord will display his glory, the splendor of our God.* In light of what we have been discussing, a remarkable admonition comes. *With this news, strengthen those who have tired hands, and encourage those who have weak knees. Say to those with fearful hearts, "Be strong, and do not fear for your God is coming to destroy your enemies. He is coming to save you."* The chapter closes with these words, *Sorrow and mourning will disappear, and they will be filled with joy and gladness.*

There is hope for the hopeless. There is a road out of darkness. There is joy for the sorrowful and comfort for mourners. Don't let the fact it is a road through the desert frighten you. Walk the path and you will find what was previously a barren and bleak desert becoming the most fertile place in your life. You can do this. You can walk this road. You can emerge from your desert and be as *green as the mountains of Lebanon.* The writer of Psalms 84 describes the same phenomenon another way, *"When they walk through the Valley of Weeping, it will become a place of refreshing springs. The autumn rains will clothe it with blessings. They will continue to grow stronger, and each of them will appear before God."* The road through the desert, the path through the Valley of Weeping, they are the same path. Remain on the path. God is coming to rescue you.

Chapter 11

The Goodness of God

"Yet I am confident I will see the Lord's goodness
while I am here in the land of the living."
Psalm 27:13

Confidence and sight are integrally related: *I am confident* and *I will see.* These are not statements for which a person living in the dark has any reference point. Sightless people can function fairly well in familiar surroundings. They memorize where physical objects are located. They have developed walking patterns for their environment. As you watch them move about, you might mistake them for someone who can see. They have memorized the safe places. However, they have a greatly diminished ability to adapt if something has been moved without their knowledge. Sightlessness brings huge restrictions to your life. If you put a sightless person in an unfamiliar room and ask him to navigate the space unaided, he has no confidence in where to place his next step. If he chooses to move, his motions are cautious and tentative. He might choose not to move at all. In that case, he is stuck. Though I am describing the situation of a person who is physically blind, it is eerily familiar to me. My loss of vision had crippled any confidence I had previously possessed. I was emotionally and spiritually stuck, frozen in place, ruled by fear with no clue regarding my next step. I restricted myself to the few safe places where I was comfortable. Vocationally, those had to do with Bible study and teaching. Relationally, I restricted myself to my family and a few close friends. The thought of taking any type of risk was terrifying.

"Nothing can be done without hope and confidence." Those words, true as they are, carry additional weight when you understand their source. They came from the lips of Helen Keller. Helen, born in Tuscumbia, Alabama, in 1880, fell ill at the age of two. The high fever that accompanied the illness robbed her of her sight, hearing, and speech. Her life's story is nothing short of remarkable. Due to the devotion of a gifted teacher, Anne Sullivan, Helen learned to communicate via touch-lip reading, Braille, typing, and finger-spelling. After two decades of arduous work, Helen learned to speak. She graduated from Radcliffe College, Cambridge, Massachusetts, in 1904 at the age of twenty-four, the first deaf and blind person to receive a Bachelor of Arts degree from any educational institution. She went on to receive honorary doctoral degrees from Temple, Harvard, the universities of Glasgow, Scotland, Berlin, Germany, Delhi, India, and Witwatersrand in Johannesburg, South Africa. She was a celebrated author, poet, political activist, and lecturer. A list of her accomplishments would fill this book. In 1955, at the age of seventy-five, she crisscrossed Asia for five months, traveling a total of forty-thousand miles and inspiring countless thousands of people with her speeches and appearances. She worked untiringly to raise awareness regarding the physically handicapped and their needs. On June 1, 1968, Helen died in her sleep at her home in Connecticut a few weeks shy of her eighty-eighth birthday. A more amazing story would be hard to imagine.

Though physically blind, Helen discovered a secret that many sighted people never learn. In her own words, "It is a terrible thing to see and have no vision." Though she was physically blind, the eyes of her heart had amazingly keen sight. Proverbs 29:18 states, "Where there is no vision, the people perish" (KJV). Far from perishing, Helen's heart blossomed into a bouquet of fragrant life. Paul the Apostle prays for the Ephesians that "the eyes of their heart" (NIV) "will be flooded with light so that (they) can understand the confident hope he has given to those he called" (Eph. 1:18 NLT). Paul, like David, understood the link between sight and confidence, enlightenment and hope. As Ms. Keller said, you can't do anything without hope and confidence. Helen Keller possessed enlightened eyes. She lived her life with a level of confidence few have exhibited. She did so because she could see in the only way that truly matters. She could see with her heart. She once said, "I can see, and that is why I can be happy, in what you call the dark, but which to me is golden. I can see a God-made world, not a manmade world."

In the little town of Boerne, Texas, sitting on the family room sofa of a dear friend, my heart heard the voice of Jesus speak penetrating words of truth that healed my blindness. Those words opened the eyes of my understanding. They weren't simply any words spoken by anyone. They were the graceful words of Jesus, pregnant with life, words of healing and freedom, of affirming love and gracious correction. Paul's prayer for the Ephesians had transcended the ages and enveloped me. The eyes of my heart were enlightened and I was filled with a confident hope that exceeded anything I had ever known. A confidence in God regarding his ability, willingness, and intention to heal became a vital part of my being. Not only was I sure God had healed and would continue to heal my heart; I knew he would heal the hearts of others. I sensed the joy he experienced and the pleasure it brought him to rain his healing love on the soil of my life hardened by pain, ignorance, and stubbornness. It's difficult to describe the level of change that occurred within me. I was as radically different as day and night. It was, without a doubt, the most life-altering spiritual experience I have ever had. I cannot imagine a more dramatic experience than a person physically blind receiving their sight. For me, my healing was no less dramatic. A world I had never seen opened before me.

I don't mean to imply I suddenly saw everything clearly and had attained some state of perfect inner wholeness. There is much work yet to be done in my life, but that work holds no fear for me. On the contrary, I look forward to it because of the confidence I have in God's desire to heal and restore and to shape my life into the image he always intended. That shaping, however, was impossible while I stumbled in the dark, groping for solid ground and paralyzingly afraid to move, yet afraid not to move. I weighed the prospect of remaining stuck against the possibility of a fatal fall. At some point, I had to choose. In the end, desperation made my choice for me. I could no longer live like I was living. Fatal fall or not, I chose to move ahead.

I particularly identified with this translation of Psalm 27:10, *"I would have despaired if I had not believed that I would see the goodness of the Lord in the land of the living"* (NASB). Despair is a place at the bottom of the sea of hopelessness. It is a horrid feeling that will, like a black hole, suck every bit of light into it. I did not believe I would ever experience anything good again. The painful experiences of my past and my unfortunate interpretation of them had led me to the shores of that sea. Despair, like Davey Jones's locker, seemed my inevitable and permanent destination. Things would no doubt be great in the next life. Pain, sorrow, and disappointment would be a thing of the past. But what of this life? I had determined to do the best I could but my expectations were next to nothing. It pains me to admit my attitude had sunk to that level, but to deny it was other than that would be a lie.

These words of David, as so many others in this psalm, became my daily prayer, my morning and evening sacrifice. *"Yet I am confident that I will see the Lord's goodness while I am here in the land of the living."* As I stood on the shore of that sea of hopelessness, I fed the wind those words again and again. Countless times I prayed and quoted, inwardly and outwardly, David's confession. Those words became the extended hand from the edge of the cliff to which I desperately clung. I wasn't sure I had the strength to hang on. In the end, I needn't have worried. The extended hand proved stronger than my own. Though I lacked the strength to hang on, the hand hung on to me. *I will, in this life, experience God's goodness.* Gradually, the hand of God pulled me from harm's way and set me upon solid ground. This psalm coupled with the love of God rescued me from the pit of despair. *"He reached down from heaven and rescued me; he drew me out of deep waters…He lifted me out of the pit of despair, out of the mud and mire. He set my feet on solid ground and steadied me as I walked along"* (Ps. 18:16; 40:2).

The Goodness of God

The goodness of God, like the glory of God, is a term I find hard to define. You know what it is when you experience it, but how do you describe it to someone else? What is this goodness David is so confident he will not be denied in this life? What is it I am looking to experience in the land of the living that I am convinced I have not? It turns out God specifically defined his goodness for us. His description occurs in a familiar biblical story, yet I had missed it for years.

The book of Exodus recounts the deliverance of Israel from Egyptian bondage. God's primary leader in that event was Pharaoh's adopted son, Moses the Reluctant. Several miracles were required to convince him of God's call to lead God's people. Even then, he insisted on a spokesperson due to his self-perceived inability to communicate. The full story is recorded in Exodus chapters twenty to thirty-three. I'd like to offer you an abbreviated version as backdrop for an understanding of God's goodness.

God summoned Moses to Mount Sinai to meet with him. At that time, Moses was given the Ten Commandments carved in stone tablets by the finger of God. At some point, the meeting was abruptly stopped. The people of Israel had fallen into sin and Moses was instructed to descend the mountain and deal with the problem. Idolatry had broken out in the form of a golden calf that miraculously emerged from a pool of molten gold. Immorality quickly followed. Upon Moses' return, he was so disturbed by what he saw, in a fit of anger, he broke the original tablets given him by God. Due to their sin, judgment and death came to many that day in the nation of Israel.

Soon after this event God beckoned Moses once again to the mountain for a follow up meeting. This time Moses was to bring his own tablets of stone upon which God reinscribed the Ten Laws. Prior to this second ascent of Mount Sinai, a conversation occurred between Moses and God. The meeting's agenda was Moses' insistence that God accompany them to the Promised Land, something God had previously declared he would not do. Rather, he would send his angel with them, for God declared if he accompanied them he would destroy the people because of their stubbornness, sin, and rebellion. This arrangement was not satisfactory to Moses. If God didn't go with them, they weren't going. God, surprisingly to me, agreed to Moses' demand (Exod. 33:14). As an indication that God intended to keep his part of the bargain, Moses asked for a sign. Moses' request is familiar to me. I have heard this text preached on many times throughout my life. Moses' petition to God was, "Show me your glory" (Exod. 33:18). In other words, if you're truly going with us affirm your presence to me. This desire to see God, to know him at a deep level, is an experience Moses believed would inspire the faith and confidence he would need to make the impending journey and deal with the opposing forces he would encounter on the trip to the Promised Land. *"Show me your glory."* As with Moses' previous request, God grants this one as well. *"The Lord replied, 'I will make all my goodness pass before you.'"* (Exod. 33:19). Moses asked to see God's glory. God's response is to show him his goodness. Somehow, through all my readings of Scripture, that fact had escaped me.

Moses ascended the mountain and God reinscribed the stone tablets he had brought with him. God then hid Moses in a crevice of rock and fulfilled Moses' request. God showed him his glory. He caused his goodness to pass before him. Exodus 34:6-7 recounts the event. *"The LORD passed in front of Moses, calling out, 'Yahweh! The LORD! The God of compassion and mercy! I am slow to anger and filled with unfailing love and faithfulness. I lavish unfailing love to a thousand generations. I forgive iniquity, rebellion, and sin. But I do not excuse the guilty. I lay the sins of the parents upon their children and grandchildren; the entire family is affected—even children in the third and fourth generations.'"*

Moses descended the mountain a changed man. In fact, he was changed in ways he was unaware. *He wasn't aware that his face had become radiant* (Exod. 34:29). The fear it engendered in Aaron and the people is what called his attention to it, so much so, in fact, he had to cover his face with a veil when meeting with people. I had always been told he was shining with the glory of God. That is true enough, but perhaps more accurately stated he was shining with the goodness of God, the very thing God caused to pass in front of him. God's goodness is his definition of his glory.

What does that goodness look like? According to the Exodus account it looks like God calling out his own name. It isn't too often you hear someone announcing themselves. But who, other than God, is qualified to introduce him? Who knows him well enough to announce his presence and describe his being; no one but God, himself. His goodness looks like compassion and mercy, unfailing love and faithfulness, and a slowness to become angry. It bears a striking resemblance to the forgiveness of sin. It manifests itself in righteous judgment. Where forgiveness is not sought or accepted, the penalty of sin plays itself out in all its ugliness to the point of affecting successive generations. The goodness of God; perhaps it is not quite what we expected. Perhaps we were thinking more along the lines of earthly comforts and noticeable prosperity, fit bodies and fat bank accounts. Instead, God paraded his nature before Moses and declared his name, *Yahweh*, the *I AM*, not the I HAVE.

"*Yet I am confident I will see the Lord's goodness while I am here in the land of the living.*" Moses saw it. David was confident he would see it. My heart ached for it. According to God, himself, the thing we will not be denied is God, himself, which in his own words is his goodness. It is the incarnation played out again and again through each who receives him. It is participation in the divine nature (2 Pet. 1:4), indwelled by the one who paraded himself on the mountain before his servant, Moses, declaring his name and his nature. His goodness is *Himself*. His glory is *Himself*. Since the coming of Christ, he no longer displays himself to us; rather, he has chosen to live in us. God in the flesh. God in my flesh. It is the wonder of the ages, the mystery of eternity. It cannot be defined or defended. He has done what he has pleased and it has pleased him to make his home in us. Words fail to do it justice.

The apostle Paul, in reference to this incident, admonishes us to live our lives with unveiled faces (2 Cor. 3:18) so that we might reflect the glory of God to a world in desperate need of seeing it. What the people of the world need to encounter, what they need to see and experience, to taste and to touch, is the goodness of God. They will experience it as it is reflected through us. They do not need luminous light displays emanating from our faces. They need firsthand encounters with his faithfulness and mercy, his compassion and forgiveness, his love and his grace, his patience and forbearance. They need to know that God is good.

God's goodness was nothing I expected to experience again; therefore, I certainly had no plans to reflect it. My expectation was of continued hardship and trouble, but an encounter with God changed everything. He secreted me in a divine crevice and passed his goodness before me in ways I would never have dreamed. His healing love transformed my life in unanticipated and wondrous ways. So much so, I am beginning to leak God, accidentally. I can't seem to help it. If you knew the old me, you would understand how amazing that is. I'm under no illusion. It isn't me. I have come from a pit of despair. The goodness is his. The pleasure is mine.

David's invitation sings much louder than it used to. *"Taste and see that the Lord is good. Oh, the joys of those who take refuge in him!"* (Ps. 34:8) In the land of the living, I have tasted and seen that the Lord is good. It's not about deserving it, for I certainly did not and do not. It is about God's great love for me. David's words became my words. Let my words become your words. You will experience the goodness of God in this life and it will change you forever. He will teach you how to live again

Chapter 12

Patience and Courage

"Wait patiently for the Lord. Be brave and courageous.
Yes, wait patiently for the Lord."
Psalm 27:14

David's final words are his greatest challenge. His words are not suggestions. The tense of the verb is imperative. It is not up for debate. He commands us to action. For those sailing relatively calm seas, these words may seem like sage advice, words of wisdom from a battle-hardened warrior who has learned to depend on God. Through his words, we are now reaping the benefits of his hard won experience. For those seafarers, David's words are inspiring and encouraging; however, for those caught in what seems an endless storm, beaten senseless by incessant waves of trouble, David's closing words are not what we're looking to hear. An admonition to wait is not welcome news. Our *waiting* reservoir has been exhausted. At best, we are merely hanging on, and the prospects of that continuing are in doubt. The challenge to courageousness is equally discouraging. When living on survival rations, the strength for feats of courage is nonexistent. Yet David's words remain. They are no respecter of persons. They have unequal value to the recipient, depending greatly upon the condition of the hearer, but they are no less true no matter which seas you are currently sailing.

I had read these words many times in my life, but I had never heard them. My seas were not calm. My storms were raging. My waters were not simply troubled, they were tumultuous. I wasn't in the midst of a little blow, as sailors sometime refer to it. I was in the middle of a typhoon of turmoil, confusion, and pain. The survival of my little ship was in grave doubt. I found no solace, no comfort, and no hope in David's words. In fact, they increased my despair. How could I possibly embrace these words and allow them to become the life-giving commands they were intended to be? Only one way: waiting.

Patience

As obvious as it may be to say, waiting and patience are not synonymous terms. Patience is used in the verse as an adverb. The verb it modifies is *wait*. Everyone ticketed for the delayed flight must wait, but not everyone waits patiently. In my journey, the definition of the word wait had come to mean languish. Languish is defined as losing or lacking vitality; to grow weak; fail to make progress or be successful. That's what *wait* meant to me. The thought of patiently waiting was nowhere near being on my radar.

David's words in Psalm 69 lead me to believe he walked in my footsteps, or rather I in his. Listen to his anguished complaint, *"I am exhausted from crying for help; my throat is parched. My eyes are swollen from weeping waiting for my God to help me"* (Ps. 69:3). These are not the words of a spiritual giant standing strong in the face of opposition. They are the agonizing testimony of a man fighting for his life. We must not imagine patient waiting as meaning to enjoy another cold beverage and a few chips until the second half of the football game begins. Patient waiting can, and often does, involve the rending of our hearts.

Patient waiting is an indispensable aspect of our relationship with God. We must learn to do it and learn to do it well. *"I waited patiently for the Lord to help me, and he turned to me and heard my cry. He lifted me out of the pit of despair, out of the mud and mire. He set my feet on solid ground and steadied me as I walked along. He has given me a new song to sing, a hymn of praise to our God. Many will see what he has done and be amazed. They will put their trust in the Lord"* (Ps. 40:1-3). Apparently, patient waiting is something David did on more than one occasion, as he refers to it again here in Psalm 40. The results as described in this psalm are noteworthy: the turning of God toward you, the knowledge your cry is heard, and your rescue from despair. Your feet find solid ground. The songs of heaven fill your heart and mouth. As a result of your amazing deliverance, great testimony to the Lord's saving power influences others to trust in him as well. Those are outstanding results by anyone's measurement. They came about because David patiently waited for the Lord to help him.

There is another piece of the equation to consider. The object of patiently waiting is the Lord. You may patiently wait to win the lottery. Odds are you will still be waiting for that until your dying day. You may be patiently waiting for a friend or family member to bail you out of your dire situation, perhaps out of a sense of pity or family obligation. Your waiting may or may not pay off. The object of your waiting is crucial. Again we turn to David's own words for direction, *"I wait quietly before God, for my victory comes from him"* (Ps. 62:1). I know it goes without saying, yet it is important to say: God is our deliverer. He may use a number of avenues to bring that deliverance. A friend or family member may very well play a key role in your recovery. If that is so, understand it for what it is: the hand of God extended to you through others. There is no other source and there will be no other source of deliverance. It will, more than likely, occur over a much longer period than you have any desire to walk through. You may attempt escapes, but an escape is not deliverance. Escapes are temporary, humanly orchestrated, and in the end worsen our situation. Deliverance is permanent, from God, and will lead you into pastures that are greener than you can imagine. The big question, then, is how do I become a patient waiter on God? If that is an indispensable ingredient in my healing, deliverance, and recovery how can I possibly do what I know without a doubt I am incapable of? The conclusion I have come to is you must know you are loved.

Patience is a manifestation of love. Paul begins his famous treatise on love, 1 Corinthians 13, with a clearly articulated and extremely pointed statement: *without love, you are nothing.* Though your speech epitomizes eloquence and you surpass all with your rhetoric, though your faith is greater than any human's and mountains move with your words, though you are the wisest person who has breathed earthly air, you understand the very secrets of God, and your life is one of ultimate self-sacrifice, if you do not love you are nothing. There is no misunderstanding the value Paul places on love. He follows these declarations with his description of what love is. *"Love is patient"* (I Cor. 13:4). Patience is the primary manifestation of love. It occurs first on Paul's list of descriptors. I believe the proper way to understand this passage is this: *you cannot be patient if you do not know that you are loved.* It is absolutely nonnegotiable. You cannot wait patiently for the Lord if you do not know you are loved by him, the one you are waiting for.

After fifty-eight years of living, the knowledge that I am loved by God has revolutionized my life. It brought healing to years of brokenness and pain. I have come to understand in a tangible, experiential way that absolutely nothing can separate me from God's love. I have always been loved, but my understanding and experience of that love has been sporadic and incomplete. I knew the Bible declared God loved me. I had experienced His love from time to time in very real ways, but during my time of healing prayer I experienced, understood, and accepted God loved me in a way I had never done before. When I did, a healing process began in my heart and continues to this day. I see no end in sight. There is laid out before me a road of personal healing upon which I will be walking hand in hand with the lover of my soul until the day I leave this world. I am recovering what has been lost and embracing what is to come. I am discovering what it means to wait patiently for the Lord. It is not as difficult as it used to be because I know the one I am waiting for loves me for exactly who I am. He always has. He always will. I can wait for someone like that forever.

Patiently waiting on God is so critical David repeats the first phrase of the verse with added emphasis and leaves it as his last word to us. *"Yes, wait patiently for the Lord."* David's words are a compelling command. The command, however, is impossible without the precondition. You must know you are loved, but once you do a new heaven and earth begin to unfold before you. Waiting on God is accompanied by an unexpected joy, a joy that will strengthen you to do whatever the situation requires. *"Yes, wait patiently before the Lord."* The unimaginable has become the enjoyable. The improbable has become the norm. I wouldn't have believed it was possible. I am living the dream. It is not a dream restricted to a few. Like the Father of the prodigal, his arms are extended and he is running to meet you. He has nothing but love and acceptance to bestow upon you. Your speech of unworthiness is unnecessary. Your rehearsal of it was wasted time. Receive his love and return his embrace. There is a ring for your finger and a robe to clothe you. The party awaits and you're the guest of honor.

Courage

Sandwiched between David's admonitions to patient waiting are these words, *"Be brave and courageous."* Courage and faith are first cousins. In fact, if they were any more closely related they would be the same thing. I do not believe that courage can exist without faith and faith cannot be lived out without courage. Trusting God and patiently waiting for him to act will, in my estimation, be the bravest thing you will ever choose to do. In all probability, it will be the thing you feel least like doing. In your dilemma, disaster, or dis-ease, you will attempt to solve the issue yourself. That proving unsuccessful, you will most likely turn to others for help. If that attempt dissolves to dust, there are various forms of medication to which you can turn to ease the pain or escape the pressure of the moment: drugs, sex, entertainment, exercise, shopping, busyness, or food and drink; anything that will help cope with the feelings you cannot seem to shake or the painful place from which you cannot extricate yourself. The list of things with which we can distract ourselves is seemingly endless in the western world. Waiting patiently for the Lord to come to our aid is probably not at the top of very many people's list. It requires the highest levels of courage and bravery to exercise that option.

Courage is not the absence of fear. In fact, courage only surfaces in the presence of fear. One of my favorite stories to illustrate this point is the deeds of the Cowardly Lion in *The Wizard of Oz.* He joined Dorothy, the Tin Man, and the Scarecrow on their journey to Oz in hopes the mighty wizard would give him courage. His hopes were disastrously dashed when instructed by the wizard that he must be party to conquering the Wicked Witch of the West in order for his wish to be granted. That very quest provided the opportunity for courage to arise, courage he had always possessed but to which he was totally oblivious. It surfaced because he loved someone else more than he loved himself. In the face of danger, courage arose and he defended someone he cared for deeply. Dorothy's safety became more important to him than his own. Upon the defeat of the witch and the return to Oz, these are the words of the transplanted Kansas wizard to the Cowardly Lion. "As for you, my fine friend—you're a victim of disorganized thinking. You are under the unfortunate delusion that simply because you run away from danger, you have no courage. You're confusing courage with wisdom. Back where I come from, we have men who are called heroes. Once a year, they take their fortitude out of mothballs and parade it down the main street of the city. And they have no more courage than you have. But! They have one thing that you haven't got! A medal! Therefore, for meritorious conduct, extraordinary valor, conspicuous bravery against wicked witches, I award you the Triple Cross. You are now a member of the Legion of Courage!"

The Lion was "a victim of disorganized thinking." He was confused. He suffered the same thing from which I suffered: a warped perspective. I had misinterpreted the events of my life for years, which, in turn, shaped my thinking about myself and created a filter through which I processed what I heard others say to me. I, like the Cowardly Lion, was "a victim of disorganized thinking." What I needed to hear was the truth, that which had been the truth all along but to which I was blinded. David's words became that truth for me. His words became a beacon of light that pierced my darkness. David offers reasons in Psalm 27 why we should not be afraid: God is our light, God is our salvation, God is our fortress protecting us from danger. He states in verse three, *"Though a mighty army surrounds me, my heart will not be afraid."* These are words to which I clung. I kept them close to my heart. I memorized them. Multiple times throughout the day I allowed them to pass my lips. They became anchors holding me steady until the storm passed, until my heart was healed. As I look back, I wonder, like the Cowardly Lion, where I got the courage. I believe the answer is desperation. In the same way as necessity is the mother of invention, desperation is the mother of courage. I realize there have been others who, in desperate situations, have acted other than courageously. Some have, in fact, acted despicably, but that does not negate the fact that it is in the face of desperation that courage has the opportunity to arise. In the face of desperation, the Cowardly Lion rose to the occasion and acted bravely. Certainly not without a level of fear that bordered on terror, yet he acted just the same. I believe it was desperation that drove me to the same choice.

It seems reasonable to me that acting courageously once in your life should be sufficient. Apparently, that was not true for David. These are his words on another occasion, *"My heart pounds in my chest. The terror of death assaults me. Fear and trembling overwhelm me and I can't stop shaking"* (Ps. 55:4-5). David knew what it was like to be afraid. I believe that is why we find so many declarations in the psalms advocating fearlessness, *"I will not fear"* (Ps. 118:6), *"I will fear no evil"* (Ps. 23:4), and many more such statements. These were not words of wishful thinking. These were weapons in his mouth against the fear that assaulted him. It is the reason I am such an advocate of using the words of Psalm 27, or another portion of scripture, as a weapon of assault against the one who seeks to destroy your life, who seeks to deprive you of fully being the person God has created you to be. David's definitive word on the subject is Psalm 34:4, *"I prayed to the Lord and he answered me. He freed me from **all** my fears."* David was a man of many fears. In the end, however, none of them permanently conquered him. Make no mistake about it, it was a war. The words with which he closes Psalm 27 are not idle chatter. *"Be* *brave and courageous."* Waiting patiently for the Lord can only be done by heroes, those who in the face of all odds stand firm. In the face of fear and desperation, they cling to the One who loves them more than is reasonable.

As I was preparing for a men's meeting, I was considering a familiar passage of scripture in which I discovered unfamiliar content. The first eight verses of Revelation 21 contain a description of the new heaven and earth we will one day inhabit. It is described as containing no tears, death, sorrow, or pain. God will be living directly among his people in ways we are yet incapable of understanding. Everything will be new. The water of life flows freely for all who are thirsty. It is an amazing and deeply appealing description of what awaits us.

The passage closes with a catalog of those who *will not* be there. It contains an expected list of suspects: unbelievers, the corrupt, murderers, the immoral, those who practice witchcraft, idol worshippers, and liars. It also contains another genre of people. It was, for me, an unexpected group to be found on the list. It was, to my surprise, first in the list of offenders: cowards (Rev. 21:8). I had never noticed this before. It came at a time in my life that I desperately needed to be brave and courageous. It was, along with other experiences I had at the time, a huge wake up call. Cowards do not inhabit the remarkable place God has prepared for his people.

This particular word for coward in its original language occurs only three times in the New Testament: Revelation 21:8, Matthew 8:26, and Mark 4:40. Both of the Gospel passages are the words of Christ. In Revelation, the words are spoken by *the one sitting on the throne* who calls himself *the Alpha and Omega—the Beginning and the End.* It seems clear to me the speaker there is also Christ. That means Jesus is the only one in the New Testament to use this word for coward. The setting for the Gospel passages is a storm on the Sea of Galilee in which Jesus and his followers find themselves.

The storm is fierce. Jesus, however, is asleep. He is awakened by the disciples because they fear for their lives. Christ's words to them in both passages are almost identical. *"Why are you afraid (cowards)? You have so little faith"* (Matt. 8:26). *"Why are you afraid (cowards)? Do you still have no faith?"* (Mark 4:40). My translation: *Why don't you believe? Why don't you have faith? Why don't you trust me? Why are you being cowards?* Jesus is clearly associating lack of trust and lack of faith with cowardice. It is cowardly not to trust him. Those who will join him in that marvelous place he is preparing for us are those who exhibit the courage to believe.

David's words in the last verse of this psalm are critical to our walk with Christ. *Be brave. Be courageous. Wait patiently for the Lord.* In the face of fear, be brave. In moments of despair, be courageous. At those times when all you want to do is run and not look back, wait patiently for the Lord. Wrap your arms around the declarations, promises, the honesty and hopes of this psalm and believe. Many times my statement of belief has been that of the man with the demon possessed son. When questioned by Jesus if he believed he could deliver his son, the man responded, *"Lord, I believe. Help my unbelief"* (Mark 9:24). Through my darkest moments, that was often the only answer I was able to offer. Yet, as in the case of the man with the demon possessed son, it was enough. It is enough.

Within you resides the courage to respond to God in faith, trust, and patient waiting. Allow your desperation to drive you to him, not away from him. You are braver than you know. In fact, a hero lives inside of you. You're a member of the Legion of Courage. You just may not know it yet.

Chapter 13

Word of God

"For the word of God is living and active,
sharper than any two-edged sword,
piercing to the division of soul and of spirit,
of joints and of marrow, and discerning
the thoughts and intentions of the heart."
Hebrews 4:12

"It's a big book, full of big stories with big characters. They have big ideas (not least about themselves) and make big mistakes. It's about God and greed and grace; about life, lust, laughter, and loneliness. It's about birth, beginnings, and betrayal; about siblings, squabbles, and sex; about power and prayer and prison and passion...And that's only Genesis."[25] N. T. Wright is one of the many authors who have written brilliantly about the word of God and its power. As I considered including a chapter regarding this subject, a keen awareness of my poverty-stricken vocabulary became painfully obvious. I did not possess the words needed to adequately describe the manner in which God's word powerfully worked in me during the dark season through which I had just passed. There seemed nothing within my literary grasp to do it justice. The immense impact of the power of God's word defies description. Nevertheless, I felt compelled to make an attempt. To do otherwise seemed cowardly.

Any attempt at a description of the power of God's word must, in my estimation, begin with a consideration of the Incarnation, the grandest mystery of the universe. We use the word *incarnate* to describe the act of God becoming man, the divine clothing itself with human form. John described it as *"the Word became flesh"* (John 1:14 ESV). God and his word are synonymous and inseparable. You cannot speak of one without speaking of the other. To have an experience with the word of God is to have an experience with God. To have an experience with God is to have an experience with his word. The writer of Hebrews describes it as *"living and active."* The *Message* renders Hebrews 4:12-13 in this manner: *"His powerful Word is sharp as a surgeon's scalpel, cutting through everything, whether doubt or defense, laying us open to listen and obey. Nothing and no one is impervious to God's Word. We can't get away from it—no matter what."*

Theresa of Avila observed, "The words of the Lord are like acts wrought in us."[26] God's words are not static, but dynamic; not lifeless, but life-giving. Yet, his word does not work the same in all. God's words in the hands of the Pharisees became letters that killed; in Paul's hands, they were filled with the life of the Spirit (see 2 Cor. 3:6). N. T. Wright observes, "The Bible isn't there simply to be an accurate reference point for people who want to look things up and be sure they've got them right."[27] The Bible is not a textbook that exists for the purpose of preparing for a final exam. Passing or failing is not the issue. God's word is the living, breathing presence of divine being. It is too impersonal to call it a force, though its forcefulness will one day radically renew the heavens and earth as we presently know them. When God's word enters your spirit, infiltrates your being, its power is brought to bear upon your life. It pierces, discerns, and divides at the deepest levels of your soul. It washes over the shores of your life like unrelenting waves of the sea. There is no part of you it will leave untouched.

As I labored through this difficult time of my life, I immersed myself in Psalm 27 again and again. Paul's words regarding being *"washed by the cleansing of God's word"* (Eph. 5:26) took on new meaning. Pain and untruth were, incrementally, swept away layer by layer. The process continues. The experience is no less real for my inability to adequately describe it. In fact, it adds a mystery to the process that carries the fragrance of God. It is an experience beyond our human capacity to imitate or define. The veracity of my experience is beyond question. My lack of ability to relay it to you in terms that can be grasped is, at the same time, frustrating and comforting; frustrating because I have a deep desire to write words so compelling that you will be unable to resist immersing yourself in God's life-giving word as handed down to us through the Bible; comforting in the fact that it is beyond my ability to do so and therefore rests safely in God's hands where it rightly belongs.

My audience for this book may be primarily Christian. Recommending the word of God to you as a source of strength and healing may be tantamount to preaching to the choir. Nevertheless, I have taken the time to champion the power of the word to you anyway, because, as a card carrying member of that choir, I experienced God's word at a level surpassing anything I had previously known. The power of God's word gripped my heart. As *The Message* so aptly puts it, I couldn't *get away from it—no matter what.* I discovered a power in the verbally spoken, often repeated, and constantly revisited passages of Scripture which altered the course of my life. I am not suggesting Psalm 27 is that word for you. I am suggesting there are words in the Bible that have been written by the finger of God and purposely placed there to revolutionize your life, heal your heart, and bring freedom to any area of bondage that may be present. If you are struggling in any part of your life and have, thus far, not found the relief, freedom, or healing you are seeking, I would like to offer a few suggestions in regards to your relationship to God's word.

First, ask God to give you an ability to read it with new eyes. Ask him to allow you to read it as though it were the first time you ever laid eyes on it. Let all preconceived notions regarding its meaning or application dissipate. Open the eyes of your heart and read. Allow God to speak to you in any way he chooses. May Paul's prayer for the Ephesians stretch across the centuries and find fulfillment in you. *"I keep asking that the God of our Lord Jesus Christ, the glorious Father, may give you the Spirit of wisdom and revelation, so that you may know him better. I pray that the eyes of your heart may be enlightened in order that you may know the hope to which he has called you, the riches of his glorious inheritance in his people, and his incomparably great power for us who believe"* (Eph. 1:17-19 NIV). God can and will enlighten the eyes of your heart in order that you may receive every life-giving syllable he has for you.

Second, journal what you hear him say. I'm not suggesting you do that simply because it was part of my journey. I am suggesting it because you will forget. It's one of the downsides of our fallen humanity. We forget. Things get lost in the ninety percent of our brain that scientists say we don't use. You do not want to forget the things God reveals to you from his Word. You will find the need to return to them in the future. That may be difficult to do if you have not recorded them. You will find their meaning and application in your life grow through time. You will live with those words like children, watching them grow and mature before your eyes. Write them down. You will never regret that you did.

Third, do not limit your exposure to a particular passage of Scripture to a single encounter. I lived in Psalm 27 for a year. I feel as if I could live in it for another year. It contains layers of truth and power that would take me the rest of my life to uncover. I have and do read other passages of Scripture. Psalm 27, however, has become a foundational stone in my life that will never be moved. Its words have become me. To extricate them would be to remove my heart from my body. Do not leave a passage of Scripture until you sense God is through speaking to you for the time being. Wait patiently for God in his word. You will not be disappointed.

Fourth, memorize the passages that are noticeably meaningful to you. Initially, that might seem a daunting task to consider. I assure you, it is not. At some point, I realized I wanted access to Psalm 27 at a moment's notice. The best way for that to happen was to hide it in my heart. A day at a time, a week at a time, I made the verses a permanent part of my daily life. In a shorter time than I imagined, the words became me and I became the words. They are indelibly etched in my soul. They are much like the hero who dove into the lake and saved your drowning child. You never forget that person. I will never forget these words.

Finally, use the words of God as a weapon against all that opposes you—the enemies of despair, depression, unbelief, bitterness, guilt, distrust, shame, loneliness, abandonment, and fear, just to name a few. As they raise their ugly heads and flash their gleaming swords, the words of God will put them to flight. It is a battle and has all the markings of a battle, including standing your ground in the face of seemingly insurmountable odds wondering if fear will win the day and you will retreat to the safety of cover. The words of God are not magic but they are mystical. It works at a level we often do not have eyes to see, but know without a doubt it is a power like no other. It *"is living and active, sharper than any two-edged sword."* Paul declares, *"The weapons we fight with are not the weapons of the world. On the contrary, they have divine power to demolish strongholds. We demolish arguments and every pretension that sets itself up against the knowledge of God, and we take captive every thought to make it obedient to Christ"* (2 Cor. 10:4-5 NIV). Don't underestimate the power of the quoted Word, internally or externally. You are called to fight. You must fight. Your weapons are the words of God as wielded by the Holy Spirit within you.

The word of God has played a vital and powerful role in my healing. Those words continue to play an integral part of my journey to emotional wholeness. That being said, it was not a quick process. Its effect has been gradual and accumulative. His Word will be a lamp for your feet and a light for your path, a light that is essential to the journey before you. David's admonition in the last verse of Psalm 27 to *"wait patiently"* is especially significant in regards to your relationship with God's word. The word of God is not a fast food drive through window. It is a five-star kitchen in which God's best for your life is painstakingly prepared. A meal like that takes time, but is worth every minute spent in preparation.

David said, *"The words of the Lord are flawless, like silver purified in a crucible, like gold refined seven times"* (Ps. 12:6 NIV). God's word is flawless. There is nothing in the entire universe with which to compare it. The universe itself was spoken into existence by words from his mouth. His very breath, the vehicle of spoken word, brought life to humankind as he breathed spirit into the nostrils of Adam. Psalm 107:20 declares, *"He sent out his word and healed them"* (NIV). According to the verses just prior, those he healed were afflicted, troubled, and distressed. His word can and will heal you. Wrap God's words around you like a cloak. They will shield you from the brutal winds of life. They will provide you with warmth on cold and lonely days. They will hide you from the enemy's eyes. In your moments of deepest desperation, the word of God will breathe life into your deflated spirit.

John the Beloved, brother of James, wrote these words from the prison island of Patmos, exiled there because of his faith in Christ, *"Then I saw heaven opened, and a white horse was standing there. Its rider was named Faithful and True, for he judges fairly and wages a righteous war. His eyes were like flames of fire, and on his head were many crowns. A name was written on him that no one understood except himself. He wore a robe dipped in blood, and his title was the Word of God"* (Rev. 19:11-13). God's word stands battle ready, eyes of fire and crowned with all authority. The robe he wears is consecrated in his own blood. His name is beyond our ability to understand, but his title is not. He is the Word of God. The Word of God will win the day. Jesus, the Word of God himself, the Word become flesh, made this declaration, *"Heaven and earth will pass away, but my words will never pass away"* (Matt. 24:35 NIV).

I leave you with the words of Hezekiah, king of Israel, as recorded by the prophet Isaiah. These words come from the lips of Hezekiah on the heels of a period of serious illness. He thought his life was over, as I did mine. I pray they are words of hope to which you can cling, words that will fill you with the strength and courage you need to challenge the darkness and emerge into the light of a new day.

I thought for sure in the prime of my life
that I'd been brought to the gates of death,
that I'd miss out on the rest of my years.
I thought: That's it. I will never again see the Eternal
in the land of the living. I will never again enjoy the company of those
alive in this world. My time on earth is folded up and packed away
like a shepherd's tent.
It's as if a weaver has snipped me off from the loom
and rolled me up. From day to night You bring

my life to an end. I stay calm until morning arrives, then like a lion
He breaks all my bones. From day to night
You bring my life to an end.
Oh, how I argue and mourn for my passing life!
Like a swallow or a crane I twitter;
like a lonesome dove I moan.
My eyes become bleary from looking
up to the heavens for help.
I cry, "O Lord, way up high, I am oppressed;
come and help me!"
But what can I say? God has spoken to me.
Things are as He made them. But I so wanted to live!
So I prayed, "Lord, by these things, people live and my spirit is
grounded in the same. So heal me, let me live!"
Paradoxically, my bitter experience
was pushing me toward wholeness.
For You, God, have put behind all
my shortcomings and wrongdoings.
You have rescued me from death.
You pulled me from a black hole of nothingness
and held me close to You.
And so I join the living in giving thanks to You.
After all, thankful voices never rise from the land of the dead.
After all, the songs of praise never soar from death's dark realm.
Those who go down into the pit— that great black nothingness—
They can't even begin to hope for Your faithfulness.
But ah, the living! And I am among them today, giving praise and
thanks to You for life, the old telling the young about the loyalty of
Your love. The Eternal will rescue me,
and we will break out the stringed instruments.
We will sing and make music for the rest of our lives,
right here in the house of the Eternal.

Isaiah 38:10-20 *The Voice Bible*

Afterword

I hope I have not left the impression that all is now right with the world, there is great joy in Mudville, and emotionally I am living comfortably on a lush tropical island enjoying gentle ocean breezes. That is simply not the case. My life has changed dramatically for the better. Deep wounds that I have carried for decades have been healed. Vision and purpose for living have been restored. These things are true. What is also true is everything in my past in need of resolution has not yet been addressed. Difficult situations I continue to face sometimes trigger past pain. The trigger turns out to be a gift, for it often reveals pain that I was unaware existed. It gives me the opportunity, but not a guarantee, to deal with it. The revelation of past pain is not the same thing as the resolution of it. I still find myself at times reluctant to go there. Why? Because it is work. To be honest, sometimes I don't want to do the work that is necessary to face my past and deal with my issues. Perhaps it's because I have too much on my plate at the time, or I am afraid of what it will uncover, or I'm just too lazy at the moment to put out the effort. Whatever the reason, there are moments, despite the healing joy I have experienced, I don't want to deal with my stuff.

During the course of writing this book, I have had seasons when old feelings of hopelessness, despair, and depression have assaulted me. I am not talking about a mild wave washing up on the beach, but a crashing breaker that causes me to question whether any healing has actually taken place in my life. I was hoping that experience was gone for good. There is a chance this is not coming across to you as good news. I certainly understand if that is your reaction. However, it is important to understand that even though heart healing has happened and will continue to happen, the journey to wholeness will last the remainder of our lives. We will not always react positively to the challenges we have yet to face. Difficulties will not always bring the best out of us. In this life, we will continue to have trouble.

I deal with my issues much differently now than I did in the past. I have tools at my disposal I did not previously possess. I have an understanding of God's love for me rooted deep within my soul. It is a place I can return and re-experience. It is not always an automatic response to revisit that place. It often requires a conscious decision, but a decision that always brings comfort and strength in trying moments.

I have a new understanding of God's word and its power to combat the assault of the enemy and the negative feelings that assail my heart and mind. Destructive thoughts can be taken captive. Lies can be confronted with an authority that is rooted in reality. I am not referring to arrogantly slinging some scriptures at the issue and expecting it to melt like a snowball on a July day in Arizona. I am referring to words of God that have penetrated our soul, and lodged in our bones. They have taken root within us. We have become them and they have become us. The word has become flesh within us, incarnated in our being. It is a powerful force combatting the lies of the enemy and releasing the comfort of the Holy Spirit.

I have learned how to keep my finger off the magic button. God is my protector. I find shelter and safety in him. It is, however, still something I must choose. In moments of pain, confusion, and emotional upheaval it is still my choice whether I will run to him or choose another option. That choice will always remain with me. Choosing God as my fortress and defender as quickly as possible is always the best option. I am, however, sometimes pretty slow on the draw. If I leave this powerful weapon in my holster for too long, I find myself sliding into a vortex of self-pity from which it is difficult to escape.

I have learned to put my cards on the table as quickly as possible. Being honest about my emotions in a safe place with safe people is an absolute necessity. Because I stuffed my emotions for so many years, it is easy to slip back toward that path if I am not diligently on guard against it. We desperately need each other as we continue to pursue a healthy and emotionally whole life.

I have had some rocky moments since my time in Boerne, Texas. In fact, it is a rocky moment I am currently in that prompts me to write these words today. It seemed an opportune time to make the point. The healing I have experienced is without a doubt the most extraordinary thing I have experienced as a Christian. The life of joy, peace, and purpose it has opened for me has been a gift from God. Ian Bradley, taking his cue from a study of early Celtic Christianity, likens life to a pilgrimage. To that end he says, "Pilgrimage…is at least as much about travelling hopefully as about arriving."[28] Life is about the journey, not the destination. If your goal is to be totally whole and you spend every waking moment dedicated to that end, there is a good possibility that you will miss the joy of living today. The totality of our wholeness will not be attained in this life. All of our brokenness will not be mended. God refused, after three impassioned pleas, to remove Paul's thorn in the flesh. It turns out it served a purpose that advanced the kingdom and honored God (2 Cor. 12:8-10). I don't want to live with pain in my life any more than you do, but pain is a part of the life we are called to live. It is unavoidable. What is avoidable is making destructive choices as we experience and deal with pain. Whether the pain is my fault, your fault, or God's fault, it is important we do not allow it to have the last word in our lives. It is important we do not permit it to blind us to the truth of God's word and the integrity of his character. As a goal, perfection, in and of itself, is an empty one. Living a life of honesty and courage in the face of pain is a worthy one. You do not have to do it alone. God will journey with you. Fellow pilgrims will come alongside.

Recently, just before going to bed one evening, I wrote the following words. I believe they are a true reflection of my heart. If that is so, the reflection is entirely due to the work of a healing God. I pray you find hope and comfort as you read them.

The Treasured Way

When I'm wounded, God, I want to bleed your heart.
Your gracious mercy like a stream flowing out of pain,
Out of my brokenness, out of my wounded heart,
A river of your love flowing gently, flowing free.
Wounds are the starting point, unlikely as it seems.
Wounds are the source for healing grace to flow
To fissures deep within the soul,
To places where the darkness lives and sorrow tries to hide.
Wounds erupt with healing balm most often for another.
The reverse, it seems, should be the truth.
The balm should be for you, but instead of being tended to
You are transformed into a source of hope,
A well of recovery for those within your reach,

But only if you choose it.
Healing help, redemptive words,
fountains of refreshing rain,
These are the things that God intends to rise out of our pain.
It seems counterintuitive, yet it is the way of love and truth.
It is the hidden, higher way, a non-insistent higher way.
I really shouldn't be surprised. It was the way of Christ.
Thorn pierced brow, spear pierced side,
nail pierced hands and feet.
Healing flowed from stripes, and pain, and brokenness.
The way was unexpected, but redemption nonetheless sprang
out of barrenness.
In the end, he was alone, in the darkness, left alone...
and then the throne.
This is territory unexplored by most,
a journey often un-embarked,
A path that is not obvious, and yet the treasured way.
It leads to unimagined heights,
peaks beyond our human view.
I hope I choose this way. I know it is the better way.
I pray that I will choose it for my own.
To bleed the heart of God...and then the throne.

Danny Mullins   August 2013

Acknowledgements

I have always felt I would write a book. I never, however, imagined it would be about the present subject. Life is full of surprises. This book certainly qualifies as a surprise for me. As obvious as it is to say, books don't write themselves. People do. And people are shaped by other people. I'd like to acknowledge some of those who have shaped my life.

Desmond Tutu said, "You don't choose your family. They are God's gift to you." It is the gift of family that has made this book possible. Without them by my side through the darkness I have passed, I would not have a tale of healing to tell.

Janet, for over four decades you have faithfully stood by my side. You are God's greatest gift to me. Your patience, love, and support have been unflagging through my disappointments, disillusionments, and defeats. I don't know how to sufficiently thank you for that. You are the love of my life. Not only the love you have shown me, but your love for others and your servant's heart continue to inspire me to grow in my own love. Thank you for being my wife, lover, and friend.

I am the blessed father of four sons, Joshua, Daniel, John, and Jacob; the fortunate father-in-law of Doni and Chimene; the peacock-proud grandfather of Jonathan and Nathan, and at ten o'clock this morning I held in my arms our two-hours-old third grandson, Jadon Joseph Mullins. You are all amazing gifts of God to me. Sharing your lives with me has left your fingerprints on this book. Thank you for being my family. Thank you for loving me. This book is for you. I hope the truths I have learned will become beacons of light for the road you are traveling.

I have chosen not to offer a list of the names of the many friends who have unwaveringly stood with me through thick and thin. Unintentionally, I would fail to mention someone deserving to be honored; therefore, I have chosen to honor you as a group. I know who you are. My heart is full of gratitude for your love and friendship. Few people are blessed with as many good friends as I have been. Your contribution to my life and to this book is priceless. Thank you.

There is one exception I want to make to the last paragraph: Barb Nelson. The three days I spent at your home in Boerne, Texas, have revolutionized my life. You are a channel through which God's healing love has found unrestricted flow. I will never forget those three days. God bless you for all the years you have spent ministering to so many others who, just like me, had lost their emotional bearings. You have helped us get our lives back on course. I am, perhaps presumptuously, speaking for everyone. Thank you from us all.

Lastly, this book is a much better book than it would have ever been due to the loving attention given to it by my editor, Kim Engel-Pearson. It was a pleasure working with you, Kim. I am deeply grateful for your help.

Danny Mullins
October 14, 2013

Appendix

I have gathered passages from Psalms I hope you will find helpful in your journey from darkness to light, from pain to joy. Some of the passages are listed to reflect our broken condition. The authors of the psalms experienced the same trouble, pain, turmoil, and confusion we all do and God has seen fit to keep an account of their struggles. Some of the passages are listed as a response to our situation. Some will bring comfort. Others will be used as weapons to combat the pain, loneliness, despair, or discouragement we face. These are real words written by real people who faced the same feelings that we face: loss, hopelessness, and destructive thoughts. May you find God's help and healing through what they have written. The list is not intended to be exhaustive. I'm sure you will discover additional passages to add to this list. I have separated them into categories for ease of reference. May God bless the reading of his word to your heart.

Abandonment

10:1   O Lord, why do you stand so far away? Why do you hide when I am in trouble?

22:1-3a My God, my God, why have you abandoned me? Why are you so far away when I groan for help? ²Every day I call to you, my God, but you do not answer. Every night you hear my voice, but I find no relief. ³Yet you are holy.

13:1-2 O Lord, how long will you forget me? Forever? How long will you look the other way? ²How long must I struggle with anguish in my soul, with sorrow in my heart every day? How long will my enemy have the upper hand?

37:28   For the Lord loves justice, and he will never abandon the godly. He will keep them safe forever.

38:8   I am exhausted and completely crushed. My groans come from an anguished heart.

38:2-22 Do not abandon me, O Lord. Do not stand at a distance, my God. ²²Come quickly to help me, O Lord my savior.

44:23-24 Wake up, O Lord! Why do you sleep? Get up! Do not reject us forever. ²⁴Why do you look the other way? Why do you ignore our suffering and oppression?

88:13-14 O Lord, I cry out to you. I will keep on pleading day by day. ¹⁴O Lord, why do you reject me? Why do you turn your face from me?

Accusation

4:2   How long will you people ruin my reputation? How long will you make groundless accusations? How long will you continue your lies?
18:43   You gave me victory over my accusers.

Anger

37:8-9 Stop being angry! Turn from your rage! Do not lose your temper— it only leads to harm. ⁹For the wicked will be destroyed, but those who trust in the Lord will possess the land.

Brokenhearted

34:8   The Lord is close to the brokenhearted; he rescues those whose spirits are crushed.

Confidence

108:1   My heart is confident in you, O God; no wonder I can sing your praises with all my heart!

112:6-8 Such people will not be overcome by evil. Those who are righteous will be long remembered. [7]They do not fear bad news; they confidently trust the Lord to care for them. [8]They are confident and fearless and can face their foes triumphantly.

Death

18:4-5 The ropes of death entangled me; floods of destruction swept over me. The grave wrapped its ropes around me; death laid a trap in my path.

68:20   Our God is a God who saves! The Sovereign Lord rescues us from death.

Despair/Distress

39:13   Leave me alone so I can smile again before I am gone and exist no more.

40:2   He lifted me out of the pit of despair, out of the mud and the mire. He set my feet on solid ground and steadied me as I walked along.

42:5-6 Why am I discouraged? Why is my heart so sad? I will put my hope in God! I will praise him again—my Savior and [6]my God! Now I am deeply discouraged, but I will remember you.

56:8   You keep track of all my sorrows. You have collected all my tears in your bottle. You have recorded each one in your book.

57:6   My enemies have set a trap for me. I am weary from distress. They have dug a deep pit in my path, but they themselves have fallen into it.

59:16   But as for me, I will sing about your power. Each morning I will sing with joy about your unfailing love. For you have been my refuge, a place of safety when I am in distress.

61:1-2   O God, listen to my cry! Hear my prayer! ²From the ends of the earth, I cry to you for help when my heart is overwhelmed.

65:3   Though we are overwhelmed by our sins, you forgive them all.

69:1-3   Save me, O God, for the floodwaters are up to my neck. ²Deeper and deeper I sink into the mire; I can't find a foothold. I am in deep water, and the floods overwhelm me. ³I am exhausted from crying for help; my throat is parched. My eyes are swollen with weeping, waiting for my God to help me.

73:2   But as for me, I almost lost my footing. My feet were slipping, and I was almost gone.

77:1-3   I cry out to God; yes, I shout. Oh, that God would listen to me! ²When I was in deep trouble, I searched for the Lord. All night long I prayed, with hands lifted toward heaven, but my soul was not comforted. ³I think of God, and I moan, overwhelmed with longing for his help.

79:8   Let your compassion quickly meet our needs, for we are on the brink of despair.

88:18   You have taken away my companions and loved ones. Darkness is my closest friend.

102:1-2 (*A prayer of one overwhelmed with trouble, pouring out problems before the Lord.*) ¹Lord, hear my prayer! Listen to my plea! ²Don't turn away from me in my time of distress. Bend down to listen, and answer me quickly when I call to you.

118:5-6 In my distress I prayed to the Lord, and the Lord answered me and set me free. ⁶The Lord is for me, so I will have no fear. What can mere people do to me?

Doubt

94:19   When doubts filled my mind, your comfort gave me renewed hope and cheer.

Enemies

3:1   O Lord, I have so many enemies; so many are against me. So many are saying, God will never rescue him.

3:6   I am not afraid of ten thousand enemies who surround me on every side.

5:8   Lead me in the right path, O Lord, or my enemies will conquer me.

6:7   My eyes are worn out because of all my enemies.

7:6   Arise, O Lord in anger! Stand up against the fury of my enemies.

9:3   My enemies retreated. They staggered and died when you appeared.

9:6   The enemy is finished, in endless ruins.

18:18   They attacked me at a moment when I was in distress, but the Lord supported me.

18:9   He rescued me because he delights in me.

18:37   I chased my enemies and caught them. I did not stop until they were conquered.

18:48   You hold me safe beyond the reach of my enemies; you save me from violent opponents.

21:8-9   You will capture all your enemies. Your strong hand will seize all who hate you. You will throw them in a flaming furnace when you appear.

28:5   So he will tear them down and they will never be rebuilt.

34:4-5   Bring shame and disgrace on those trying to kill me; turn them back and humiliate those who want to harm me. ⁵Blow them away like chaff in the wind— a wind sent by the angel of the Lord.

41:11   I know you are pleased with me, for you have not let my enemies triumph over me.

42:1-3   As the deer longs for streams of water, so I long for you, O God. ²I thirst for God, the living God. When can I go and stand before him? ³Day and night I have only tears for food, while my enemies continually taunt me, saying, "Where is this God of yours?"

42:9-10   "O God my rock," I cry, "Why have you forgotten me? Why must I wander around in grief, oppressed by my enemies?" ¹⁰Their taunts break my bones. They scoff, "Where is this God of yours?"

44:5 Only by your power can we push back our enemies; only in your name can we trample our foes.

53:5 Terror will grip them, terror like they have never known before. God will scatter the bones of your enemies. You will put them to shame, for God has rejected them.

54:1-7 Come with great power, O God, and rescue me! Defend me with your might. ²Listen to my prayer, O God. Pay attention to my plea. ³For strangers are attacking me; violent people are trying to kill me. They care nothing for God. ⁴But God is my helper. The Lord keeps me alive! ⁵May the evil plans of my enemies be turned against them. Do as you promised and put an end to them. ⁶I will sacrifice a voluntary offering to you; I will praise your name, O Lord, for it is good. ⁷For you have rescued me from my troubles and helped me to triumph over my enemies.

56:9 My enemies will retreat when I call to you for help. This I know: God is on my side!

57:1 Have mercy on me, O God, have mercy! I look to you for protection.

59:1 Rescue me from my enemies, O God. Protect me from those who have come to destroy me.

62:7 My victory and honor come from God alone. He is my refuge, a rock where no enemy can reach me.

66:-4 Shout joyful praises to God, all the earth! ²Sing about the glory of his name! Tell the world how glorious he is. ³Say to God, "How awesome are your deeds! Your enemies cringe before your mighty power. ⁴Everything on earth will worship you; they will sing your praises, shouting your name in glorious songs."

68:1-2 Rise up, O God, and scatter your enemies. Let those who hate God run for their lives. ²Blow them away like smoke. Melt them like wax in a fire.

81:1-3   O God, do not be silent! Do not be deaf. Do not be quiet, O God. ²Don't you hear the uproar of your enemies? Don't you see that your arrogant enemies are rising up? ³They devise crafty schemes against your people; they conspire against your precious ones.

92:10-11   But you have made me as strong as a wild ox. You have anointed me with the finest oil. ¹¹My eyes have seen the downfall of my enemies; my ears have heard the defeat of my wicked opponents.

107:2 Has the Lord redeemed you? Then speak out! Tell others he has redeemed you from your enemies.

109:21-22   But deal well with me, O Sovereign Lord, for the sake of your own reputation! Rescue me because you are so faithful and good. ²²For I am poor and needy, and my heart is full of pain.

Fear

34:4   I prayed to the Lord, and he answered me.   He freed me from all my fears

56:3-4   But when I am afraid, I will put my trust in you. ⁴I praise God for what he has promised. I trust in God, so why should I be afraid? What can mere mortals do to me?

God's Presence

16:8   I know the Lord is always with me.

16:11   You will show me the way of life, granting me the joy of your presence and the pleasures of living with you forever.

18:11   He shrouded himself in darkness, veiling his approach with dark rain clouds.

22:11   Do not stay so far from me, for trouble is near, and no one else can help me.

23:4   Even when I walk through the darkest valley, I will not be afraid, for you are close beside me.

27:8   I love your sanctuary, Lord, the place where your glorious presence dwells.

75:1   We thank you, O God! We give thanks because you are near.

84:1-2, 4   How lovely is your dwelling place, O Lord of Heaven's Armies. ²I long, yes, I faint with longing to enter the courts of the Lord. With my whole being, body and soul, I will shout joyfully to the living God...⁴What joy for those who can live in your house, always singing your praises.

100:5   For the Lord is good. His unfailing love continues forever, and his faithfulness continues to each generation.

Guidance

23:3   He guides me along right paths, bringing honor to his name.

31:3   You are my rock and my fortress. For the honor of your name, lead me out of this danger.

32:8-9   The Lord says, "I will guide you along the best pathway for your life. I will advise you and watch over you.

⁹ Do not be like a senseless horse or mule that needs a bit and bridle to keep it under control."

37:23-34 The Lord directs the steps of the godly. He delights in every detail of their lives. ²⁴ Though they stumble, they will never fall, for the Lord holds them by the hand.

40:5 O Lord my God, you have performed many wonders for us. Your plans for us are too numerous to list. You have no equal. If I tried to recite all your wonderful deeds, I would never come to the end of them.

48:14 For that is what God is like. He is our God forever and ever, and he will guide us until we die.

Hope

71:5-6 O Lord, you alone are my hope. I've trusted you, O Lord, from childhood. ⁶ Yes, you have been with me from birth; from my mother's womb you have cared for me. No wonder I am always praising you!

Joy

30:5 Weeping may last for a night, but joy comes in the morning.

30:11-12 You have turned my mourning into joyful dancing. You have taken away my clothes of mourning and clothed me with joy, ¹² that I might sing praises to you and not be silent. O Lord my God, I will give you thanks forever!

43:4 There I will go to the altar of God, to God—the source of all my joy. I will praise you with my harp, O God, my God!

68:3, 6   But let the godly rejoice. Let them be glad in God's presence. Let them be filled with joy...God places the lonely in families; he sets the prisoners free and gives them joy.

92:4   You thrill me, Lord, with all you have done for me! I sing for joy because of what you have done.

Justice

25:8   The Lord is good and does what is right.

33:4   For the word of the Lord holds true, and we can trust everything he does.

36:5-6   Your unfailing love, O Lord, is as vast as the heavens; your faithfulness reaches beyond the clouds. ⁶ Your righteousness is like the mighty mountains, your justice like the ocean depths.

Light

18:28   You light a lamp for me. The Lord my God lights up my darkness.

104:1-2 Let all that I am praise the Lord. O Lord my God, how great you are! You are robed with honor and majesty. ² You are dressed in a robe of light.

112:4   Light shines in the darkness for the godly.

Meditation

48:9   O God, we meditate on your unfailing love as we worship in your Temple.

63:6   I lie awake thinking of you, meditating on you through the night.

Patience

37:7   Be still in the presence of the Lord, and wait patiently for him to act. Don't worry about evil people who prosper or fret about their wicked schemes.

40:1   I waited patiently for the Lord to help me, and he turned to me and heard my cry.

46:10   Be still, and know that I am God!

62:1, 5   I wait quietly before God, for my victory comes from him... Let all that I am wait quietly before God, for my hope is in him.

Prayer

4:1   Answer me when I call to you, O God who declares me innocent. Free me from my troubles. Have mercy on me and hear my prayer.

5:1-3   O Lord, hear me as I pray; pay attention to my groaning. ²Listen to my cry for help, my King and my God, for I pray to no one but you. ³Listen to my voice in the morning, Lord. Each morning I bring my requests to you and wait expectantly.

6:8-10 Go away, all you who do evil, for the Lord has heard my weeping. ⁹The Lord has heard my plea; the Lord will answer my prayer. ¹⁰May all my enemies be disgraced and terrified. May they suddenly turn back in shame.

9:12   He does not ignore the cries of those who suffer.

10:17 Lord, you know the hopes of the helpless. Surely you will hear their cries and comfort them.

13:3 Turn and answer me, O Lord my God! Restore the sparkle to my eyes, or I will die.

17:1 Pay attention to my prayer, for it comes from honest lips.

22:24 For he has not ignored or belittled the suffering of the needy. He has not turned his back on them, but has listened to their cries for help.

28:1 I pray to you, O Lord, my rock. Do not turn a deaf ear to me. For if you are silent, I might as well give up and die.

39:12 Hear my prayer, O Lord! Listen to my cries for help! Don't ignore my tears.

86:1-2 Bend down, O Lord, and hear my prayer; answer me, for I need your help. Protect me, for I am devoted to you. Save me, for I serve you and trust you. You are my God.

116:1-2 I love the Lord because he hears my voice and my prayer for mercy. ² Because he bends down to listen, I will pray as long as I have breath!

Protection

11:1 I trust in the Lord for protection.

16:1 Keep me safe, O God, for I have come to you for protection.

16:5 You guard all that is mine.

31:1   O Lord, I have come to you for protection; don't let me be disgraced. Save me, for you do what is right.

31:4   Pull me from the trap my enemies have set for me, for I find protection in you alone.

55:22   Give your burdens to the Lord, and he will take care of you. He will not permit the godly to slip and fall.

71:1-3   O Lord, I have come to you for protection; don't let me be disgraced. ²Save me and rescue me, for you do what is right. Turn your ear to listen to me, and set me free. ³Be my rock of safety where I can always hide. Give the order to save me, for you are my rock and my fortress.

84:11   For the Lord God is our sun and our shield. He gives us grace and glory.

91:1-4   Those who live in the shelter of the Most High will find rest in the shadow of the Almighty. ²This I declare about the Lord: He alone is my refuge, my place of safety; he is my God, and I trust him. ³For he will rescue you from every trap and protect you from deadly disease. ⁴He will cover you with his feathers. He will shelter you with his wings. His faithful promises are your armor and protection.

91:9-12   If you make the Lord your refuge, if you make the Most High your shelter, ¹⁰no evil will conquer you; no plague will come near your home. ¹¹For he will order his angels to protect you wherever you go. ¹²They will hold you up with their hands so you won't even hurt your foot on a stone.

94:22   But the Lord is my fortress; my God is the mighty rock where I hide.

95:6-7 Come, let us worship and bow down. Let us kneel before the Lord our maker, [7] for he is our God. We are the people he watches over, the flock under his care.

121:5-8 The Lord himself watches over you! The Lord stands beside you as your protective shade. [6] The sun will not harm you by day, nor the moon at night. [7] The Lord keeps you from all harm and watches over your life. [8] The Lord keeps watch over you as you come and go, both now and forever.

Repentance

Ps 51 Have mercy on me, O God, because of your unfailing love. Because of your great compassion, blot out the stain of my sins. [2] Wash me clean from my guilt. Purify me from my sin. [3] For I recognize my rebellion; it haunts me day and night. [4] Against you, and you alone, have I sinned; I have done what is evil in your sight. You will be proved right in what you say, and your judgment against me is just. [5] For I was born a sinner— yes, from the moment my mother conceived me. [6] But you desire honesty from the womb, teaching me wisdom even there. [7] Purify me from my sins, and I will be clean; wash me, and I will be whiter than snow. [8] Oh, give me back my joy again; you have broken me—now let me rejoice. [9] Don't keep looking at my sins. Remove the stain of my guilt. [10] Create in me a clean heart, O God. Renew a loyal spirit within me. [11] Do not banish me from your presence, and don't take your Holy Spirit from me. [12] Restore to me the joy of your salvation, and make me willing to obey you. [13] Then I will teach your ways to rebels, and they will return to you. [14] Forgive me for shedding blood, O God who saves; then I will joyfully sing of your forgiveness. [15] Unseal my lips, O Lord, that my mouth may praise you. [16] You do not desire a sacrifice, or I would offer one. You do not want a burnt offering. [17] The sacrifice you desire is a broken spirit. You will not reject a broken and repentant heart,

O God. ¹⁸ Look with favor on Zion and help her; rebuild the walls of Jerusalem. ¹⁹ Then you will be pleased with sacrifices offered in the right spirit—with burnt offerings and whole burnt offerings. Then bulls will again be sacrificed on your altar.

Rescue

18:16-19   He reached down from heaven and rescued me; he drew me out of deep waters. ¹⁷ He rescued me from my powerful enemies, from those who hated me and were too strong for me. ¹⁸ They attacked me at a moment when I was in distress, but the Lord supported me. ¹⁹ He led me to a place of safety; he rescued me because he delights in me.

25:17-18   My problems go from bad to worse. Oh save me from them all. Feel my pain and see my trouble. Forgive all my sins.

30:1-3   I will exalt you, Lord, for you rescued me. You refused to let my enemies triumph over me. ² O Lord my God, I cried to you for help, and you restored my health. ³ You brought me up from the grave, O Lord. You kept me from falling into the pit of death.

31:2   Turn your ears to me; rescue me quickly.

31:15   My future is in your hands. Rescue me from those who hunt me down relentlessly.

34:6-7   In my desperation I prayed, and the Lord listened; he saved me from all my troubles. ⁷ For the angel of the Lord is a guard; he surrounds and defends all who fear him.

35:9-10   Then I will rejoice in the Lord. I will be glad because he rescues me. ¹⁰ With every bone in my body I will praise him:

"Lord, who can compare with you? Who else rescues the helpless from the strong? Who else protects the helpless and poor from those who rob them?"

37:39-40 The Lord rescues the godly; he is their fortress in times of trouble. 40 The Lord helps them, rescuing them from the wicked. He saves them, and they find shelter in him.

40:13   Please, Lord, rescue me! Come quickly, Lord, and help me.

49:15   But as for me, God will redeem my life. He will snatch me from the power of the grave.

55:16-19 But I will call on God, and the Lord will rescue me. 17 Morning, noon, and night I cry out in my distress, and the Lord hears my voice. 18 He ransoms me and keeps me safe from the battle waged against me, though many still oppose me. 19 God, who has ruled forever, will hear me and humble them.

59:9   You are my strength; I wait for you to rescue me, for you, O God, are my fortress.

70:1-2 Please, God, rescue me! Come quickly, Lord, and help me. 2 May those who try to kill me be humiliated and put to shame. May those who take delight in my trouble be turned back in disgrace.

91:14-15 The Lord says, "I will rescue those who love me. I will protect those who trust in my name. 15 When they call on me, I will answer; I will be with them in trouble. I will rescue and honor them.

94:17-18 Unless the Lord had helped me, I would soon have settled in the silence of the grave. ¹⁸ I cried out, "I am slipping!" but your unfailing love, O Lord, supported me.

106:4-5 Remember me, Lord, when you show favor to your people; come near and rescue me. ⁵ Let me share in the prosperity of your chosen ones. Let me rejoice in the joy of your people; let me praise you with those who are your heritage.

119:94 I am yours; rescue me!

119:123 My eyes strain to see your rescue, to see the truth of your promise fulfilled.

121:1-2 I look up to the mountains— does my help come from there? ² My help comes from the Lord, who made heaven and earth!

Shame

69:5-8 O God, you know how foolish I am; my sins cannot be hidden from you. ⁶ Don't let those who trust in you be ashamed because of me, O Sovereign Lord of Heaven's Armies. Don't let me cause them to be humiliated, O God of Israel. ⁷ For I endure insults for your sake; humiliation is written all over my face. ⁸ Even my own brothers pretend they don't know me; they treat me like a stranger.

Sleep

3:5-6 I lay down and slept, yet I woke up in safety, for the Lord was watching over me. I am not afraid of ten thousand enemies who surround me on every side.

4:8   In peace I will lie down and sleep, for you alone, O Lord, will keep me safe.

Strength

28:8   The Lord gives his people strength.

73:25-26 Whom have I in heaven but you? I desire you more than anything on earth. ²⁶ My health may fail, and my spirit may grow weak, but God remains the strength of my heart; he is mine forever.

86:16   Look down and have mercy on me.   Give your strength to your servant; save me, the son of your servant.

105:4   Search for the Lord and for his strength; continually seek him.

Trouble

31:7   For you have seen my troubles, and you care about the anguish of my soul.

31:9-10 Have mercy on me, Lord, for I am in distress. Tears blur my eyes. My body and soul are withering away. ¹⁰ I am dying from grief; my years are shortened by sadness. Sin has drained my strength; I am wasting away from within.

32:7   For you are my hiding place; you protect me from trouble. You surround me with songs of victory.

40:12   For troubles surround me— too many to count! My sins pile up so high I can't see my way out. They outnumber the hairs on my head. I have lost all courage.

46:1   God is our refuge and strength, always ready to help in times of trouble.

55:1-2   Listen to my prayer, O God. Do not ignore my cry for help! ² Please listen and answer me, for I am overwhelmed by my troubles.

66:12   We went through fire and flood, but you brought us to a place of great abundance.

71:20-21 You have allowed me to suffer much hardship, but you will restore me to life again and lift me up from the depths of the earth. ²¹ You will restore me to even greater honor and comfort me once again.

Ps. 75:3 When the earth quakes and its people live in turmoil, I am the one who keeps its foundations firm.

81:6   Now I will take the load from your shoulders; I will free your hands from their heavy tasks.

84:6-7   When they walk through the Valley of Weeping, it will become a place of refreshing springs. The autumn rains will clothe it with blessings. ⁷ They will continue to grow stronger, and each of them will appear before God in Jerusalem.

86:6-7   Listen closely to my prayer, O Lord; hear my urgent cry. I will call to you whenever I'm in trouble, and you will answer me.

88:1-3 O Lord, God of my salvation. I cry out to you by day. I come to you at night. ² Now hear my prayer; listen to my cry. ³ For my life is full of troubles, and death draws near.

93:3-4   The floods have risen up, O Lord. The floods have roared like thunder; the floods have lifted their pounding waves. ⁴ But mightier than the violent raging of the seas, mightier than the breakers on the shore—the Lord above is mightier than these!

107:6   "Lord, help!" they cried in their trouble, and he rescued them from their distress.

107:28-30   "Lord, help!" they cried in their trouble, and he saved them from their distress. ²⁹ He calmed the storm to a whisper and stilled the waves. ³⁰ What a blessing was that stillness as he brought them safely into harbor!

119:50   Your promise revives me; it comforts me in all my troubles.

120:1   I took my troubles to the Lord; I cried out to him, and he answered my prayer.

Truth

119:29   Keep me from lying to myself; give me the privilege of knowing your instructions.

119:160   The very essence of your words is truth.

Victory

44:3-4   They did not conquer the land with their swords; it was not their own strong arm that gave them victory. It was your right hand and strong arm and the blinding light from your face that helped them, for you loved them. ⁴ You are my King and my God. You command victories for Israel.

103:1-5   Let all that I am praise the Lord; with my whole heart, I will praise his holy name. ² Let all that I am praise the Lord; may I never forget the good things he does for me. ³ He forgives all my sins and heals all my diseases. ⁴ He redeems me from death and crowns me with love and tender mercies. ⁵ He fills my life with good things. My youth is renewed like the eagle's!

108:12-13 Oh, please help us against our enemies, for all human help is useless. ¹³ With God's help we will do mighty things, for he will trample down our foes.

116:3-9 Death wrapped its ropes around me; the terrors of the grave overtook me. I saw only trouble and sorrow. ⁴ Then I called on the name of the Lord: "Please, Lord, save me!" ⁵ How kind the Lord is! How good he is! So merciful, this God of ours! ⁶ The Lord protects those of childlike faith; I was facing death, and he saved me. ⁷ Let my soul be at rest again, for the Lord has been good to me. ⁸ He has saved me from death, my eyes from tears, my feet from stumbling. ⁹ And so I walk in the Lord's presence as I live here on earth!

118:17 I will not die; instead, I will live to tell what the Lord has done.

Weakness

6:2-3, 6-7 Have compassion on me, Lord, for I am weak. Heal me, Lord, for my bones are in agony. ³ I am sick at heart. How long, O Lord, until you restore me?... ⁶ I am worn out from sobbing. All night I flood my bed with weeping, drenching it with my tears. ⁷ My vision is blurred by grief; my eyes are worn out because of all my enemies.

Word of God

119:37 Turn my eyes from worthless things, and give me life through your word.

119:81 I am worn out waiting for your rescue, but I have put my hope in your word.

119:92 If your instructions hadn't sustained me with joy, I would have died in my misery.

119:114 You are my refuge and my shield; your word is my source of hope.

119:143 As pressure and stress bear down on me, I find joy in your commands.

119:162 I rejoice in your word like one who discovers a great treasure.

Endnotes

[1] Simone de Beauvoir, *Prime of Life* (Cambridge, MA: Da Capo Press, Inc, 1994). Quoted from http://www.goodreads.com/quotes/446217-to-be-oneself-simply-oneself-is-so-amazing-and.

[2] C. S. Lewis, *The Weight of Glory* (San Francisco, CA: Harper Collins Publishers, 2001), 46.

[3] Parker Palmer, *Let Your Life Speak* (San Francisco, CA: John Wiley and Sons, 2000), 2.

[4] Dallas Willard, *The Divine Conspiracy* (New York, NY: Harper Collins Publishers, 1998), 15.

[5] Henri Nouwen, *The Return of the Prodigal Son* (New York, NY: Image Books, 1992), 43.

[6] Palmer, 66.

[7] Gary Kinnaman and Richard Jacobs, *Seeing In The Dark* (Bloomington, MN: Bethany House, 2006), 115.

[8] Palmer, 48.

[9] Mary Sarton, "Now I Become Myself," *Collected Poems 1930-1993* (New York: W.W. Norton, 1974), 156.

[10] Palmer, 3.

[11] Søren Kierkegaard, *Journalen* (Copenhagen: Søren Kierkegaard Research Center, 1997), Volume 18, 306.

[12] Corrie Ten Boom, John and Elizabeth Sherrill, *The Hiding Place* (Grand Rapids: Chosen Books, 1971), 38.

[13] Ibid., 173.

14 Francis S. Collins and Victor A. McKusick, *Implications of the Human Genome Project for Medical Science*, February 7, 2001, http://jama.jamanetwork.com/article.aspx?articleid=193524 (accessed May 2013)

15 Peter Gena, *Selected Examples of DNA Music*, http://www.petergena.com/DNAmus.html (accessed May 2013).

16 *Music Therapy*, http://www.sickkids.ca/ProgramsandServices/ Creative-Arts-Therapy/Music-Therapy/Music-Therapy.html (accessed May 2013).

17 Constanze Letsch, *Turkish Doctors Call The Tune With Traditional Musical Cures*, August 28, 2011, http://www.theguardian.com/world/2011/aug/28/turkish-doctors-traditional-music-therapy (accessed May 2013).

18 *Music Therapy*, http://medicaldictionary.thefreedictionary.com /music+therapy (accessed May 2013)

19 Merriam Webster Online Dictionary http://www.merriamwebster.com/dictionary/ soul%20music (accessed October 9, 2013).

20 As quoted by Francis S. Collins, *The Language of God* (New York: Free Press, 2006), 33.

21 National Abortion Federation, http://www.abortionbronx.com/private-abortion.html (accessed May 2012).

22 As quoted by Goodreads, http://www.goodreads.com/quotes/8986-joy-is-the-infallible-sign-of-the-presence-of-god (accessed October 2012).

23 Ernest Lawrence Thayer,*Casey at the Bat* (New York: Putnam and Grosset, 1997), 26.

[24] Dietrich Bonhoeffer, *Life Together* (San Francisco, CA: Harper and Row Publishers, 1954), 17.

[25] N. T. Wright, *Simply Christian* (New York: HarperOne, 2006), 173.

[26] Teresa of Avila, *Interior Castle*, E. Allison Peers, ed. and trans. (New York: Image Books Doubleday, 2004), 218.

[27] Wright, 182.

[28] Ian Bradley, *Colonies of Heaven* (London: Dartman, Longman and Todd, 2000), 242.

Bible Sources

New Testament scripture quotations marked "AMP" are taken from *The Amplified Bible*, New Testament. Copyright © 1954, 1958, 1987, by The Lockman Foundation. Used by permission.

Scripture quotations marked "ESV" are taken from *The Holy Bible, English Standard Version*. Copyright © 2000; 2001 by Crossway Bibles, a division of Good News Publishers. Used by permission. All rights reserved.

Scripture quotations marked "HCSB" are taken from the *Holman Christian Standard Bible*. Copyright © 1999, 2000, 2002, 2003, by Holman Bible Publishers. Used by permission.

Scripture quotations marked "KJV" are taken from the *Holy Bible, King James Version*. Cambridge, 1769.

Scripture quotations marked "NASB" are taken from the *New American Standard Bible*, Copyright © 1960, 1962, 1963, 1968, 1971, 1972, 1973, 1975, 1977, 1995 by The Lockman Foundation. Used by permission.

Scripture quotations marked "NIV" are taken from the *Holy Bible, New International Version®. NIV®*. Copyright © 1973, 1978, 1984 by

About the Author

Danny Mullins is currently a staff pastor at Vineyard Community Church in Gilbert, Arizona. After having served as lead pastor for ten years at a congregation in his hometown of Amarillo, Texas, he has served on staff at several churches across the Southwest since entering fulltime vocational ministry in 1979. He completed a Masters of Ministry Diploma at St. Stephens University in St. Stephens, New Brunswick. He is part of the adjunct faculty at The Masters Institute in Minneapolis, Minnesota. In the past year, he has discovered a growing passion and found deep fulfillment through the ministry of inner healing prayer and spiritual direction. He has been married to his wife, Janet, since 1974, is the father of four grown sons, father-in-law of two beautiful young ladies, and is Pops to three grandsons.

To purchase additional copies of *Darkenss to Light*, or if you would like information regarding scheduling an appointment for inner healing prayer or spiritual direction, you can contact him at www.healingpresence.net.

Made in the USA
San Bernardino, CA
25 March 2017